DATE DUE

MAY 0 0 2001	

MASSACRE!

Massacre of Major Dade and his Command.

by

Frank Laumer

University of Florida Press
Gainesville

Cut on title page taken from Incidents in American History, *1847*

To My Brothers

MARSH, who taught me the fascination
of history

And
DON, whose constant encouragement
led me to writing

PREFACE

THIS BOOK is not fiction, but history. A five-year search has been made for every book, article, document, diary, and letter that makes even oblique reference to a battle which took place during the Second Seminole War and which has come to be known as Dade's Massacre. Knowledge of every action and condition recounted here is derived from a close study of the material gathered, and the few gaps discovered have been bridged with what seem to be the most logical deductions and are clearly labeled as such in the footnotes.

Incredibly enough, the name of the man whose death, more than any other single event, brought about the longest sustained war in which the United States has ever engaged —Brevet Major Francis Langhorne Dade—has not been listed in any biographical encyclopedia since the turn of the century. Only after two years of research was it possible to discover his date of birth. His exact birthplace is unknown and his grave is shared by others.

There is, of course, an explanation for this obscurity, and it lies neither in the man nor in the circumstances of his death, but in the time. Only two months after Dade's battle and before it could become fixed in the public mind another battle took place, this one in Texas. Again brave men died, but there was no subsequent event to crowd it off the stage and as a result we all "Remember the Alamo."

To dispel the long shadows that have fallen across the

men of Major Dade's command, the road they traveled, and the circumstances which determined their fate—to share a desperate moment in our history with the men who lived it—is the goal of this book.

FRANK LAUMER

At Talisman
January, 1968

ACKNOWLEDGMENTS

I WISH TO acknowledge first my debt of inspiration for the story of Dade and his command to Mr. Walter Lord, author of many excellent historical works. The evening I finished reading his *A Time to Stand,* the story of the defenders of the Alamo, I commented to my wife that someone ought to give the same research and writing treatment to Dade's Massacre. I hope that Mr. Lord will feel that my effort has been worthy of his inspiration.

During the early stages of research, December, 1963, my children Valerie and Christopher (then ages 14 and 11) accompanied me on the retracing of Dade's second day of travel (from the Little Hillsborough to the Big), a distance of some fifteen miles made longer by necessary detours. With light packs and sturdy steps they walked every foot of the way. I wish to express to them my pride and appreciation of their cheerful comradeship. I could not have had better company.

To Valerie, I am additionally grateful for her diligent search which resulted in discovery of the music for "Bruce's Address," the dirge played by Gaines' army at the burial of Dade and his command. I thank her also for the many hours of research in the *Army and Navy Chronicle* for items relating to our subject and for much time spent in typing. Her constant interest and assistance will always be remembered.

William Goza, friend, attorney, and past president of the Florida Historical Society, has rendered assistance of every type and in every way. From his own splendid collection of Florida material he made available to me original newspapers of the 1830's giving accounts of the massacre and descriptions of the Seminole chiefs. Enthusiastic with the idea from the beginning, Bill has struggled with me in the tangled thickets of the field as well as in the library. Year after year he has written, called, and visited us with a new clue, a possible lead, or words of encouragement. He has read each word of the manuscript not once but many times and improved it by his comments and suggestions. Each time that I have had the opportunity to deliver a talk on the subject of Dade (is there any other?), Bill Goza and his charming wife Sue have never failed to be in the auidence, listening with every evidence of attention. For such stout support I can only be forever grateful.

Virtually everyone to whom I have spoken during the last five years has had to listen to words about Francis Dade and his command. Literally hundreds of these people have been helpful in the search in many ways from giving specific leads to extending general encouragement. The following I must particularly mention with at least a word as to their specific contribution: the late and much missed Father Jerome of St. Leo College whose many messages in large hand-scrawl made necessary by his fading vision led the author down fruitful paths; my brother Don (Keith), a professional writer, who read and annotated the entire manuscript and whose complete confidence in its total success from inception to publication was more than gratifying; Elmer Mullins of Dade City, a professional surveyor, gave much of his time to the explanation and translation of material (the old government survey maps and modern maps) and rendered critical assistance in establishing the exact route of the old Fort King Road; the late Mrs. Helen Alexander, long the librarian of the Hugh Embry Library of Dade City, and

Mrs. Frances Hansen, her daughter and successor, who cut and hacked at red tape entanglements in successful efforts to procure reference books that otherwise would seemingly rest safely in the depths of locked vaults forever, perfectly preserved and never read; Dr. John Mahon and Dr. Sam Proctor of the University of Florida, Gainesville, read the manuscript and benefitted the author by their suggestions and by their steady encouragement. John Mahon lent further professional assistance and a strong back in the dig for evidence of the burial site. Miss Margaret Chapman of the University of South Florida Library in Tampa and Miss Elizabeth Alexander of the University of Florida Library in Gainesville both extended all the information and facilities at their command in the search for material; Rolfe Schell of Fort Myers Beach, writer and publisher, read and commented helpfully on the manuscript as did my brother-in-law William F. Brown of Tampa, West Pointer and student of Florida history; the late Dr. Rembert Patrick assisted the author through the files of the Julian Yonge collection on Florida history and afforded him the first opportunity to speak to the Florida Historical Society on the subject of the Massacre; Dr. Mark Boyd of Tallahassee, eminent Florida historian, kindly made available to the author his copy of *The Surprising Adventures of Ransom Clarke Among the Indians in Florida,* an extremely rare publication no longer available even in such prestigious collections as the Library of Congress; Baynard Kendrick of Leesburg, Florida, novelist and historian, supplied leads and encouragement; Bill Miller, Director of the Florida Board of Parks and Historic Memorials, generously gave permission for the first reopening of the grave of Dade's command since 1842 and interrupted his very crowded schedule to drive the five hundred mile round trip to the site and join in the hot and laborious task of excavation; Mrs. Eloise Ott, author and great-grandniece of Zachary Taylor, made available items in her possession that bore critically upon

the massacre; Mrs. Claire Ewertz of Titusville, Florida,
loaned several rare books that were helpful; Tom Wright,
my nephew, an inspired professional photographer, made
countless photographs at much trouble and expense that
help to illustrate the story of Dade and his command;
Mrs. Lee Claiborne Bassett, a distant relative of Francis
Dade, made many visits, wrote many letters, and supplied
much material on the genealogical history of Dade; in
Dade City, Mrs. Lilly Revell assisted with medical information and the loan of books; Mr. Rodney Cox read
the manuscript and aided by his suggestions; Dr. and Mrs.
H. E. Owen made perpetual loan of critical books and
Miss Dorothy Lock helped greatly through searching the
files of the Dade City *Banner* for pertinent material. All
of these and more gave generously of time and effort
with no reward other than the author's thanks. I hereby
acknowledge my debt to them and my deep appreciation.

In specific subdivisions of assistance I want to thank
Elmo Collins, Joe Geiger, and Jim Back who accompanied
the author along many miles of the Fort King Road,
climbing fences, slogging through the rain, and eating
endless cans of tuna fish. And I am grateful to the memory
of my faithful collie Amos who traveled five days and
nights with me on the trail of Major Dade. With instinct
and courage he warded off the malevolent attention of
countless bulls who resented the trespass through their
pastures. Without a whimper he swam cold rivers and
each night slept, tired and footsore, only to trot cheerfully
on each morning. If somewhere there is a reward for
those who have been true and loyal I trust that he has
found it.

To David Davis who now owns the deep clay pool
where Dade and his men spent their last night on earth
and who kindly allowed our bedraggled group of hikers
to camp on his property and to take refuge in his barn
from a midnight rain, I want to voice my appreciation,
as to those unknown persons who allowed us to trespass

ACKNOWLEDGMENTS xiii

through their fields, woods and backyards along the old Fort King Road.

In the matter of the weapons of the period I thank Albert Manucy of the National Park Service who answered endless questions concerning the six-pounder and without whose help it would have been impossible to write those sections covering the cannon. Milton Jones of Clearwater and Fred Bromley of Dade City supplied critical information on muskets and rifles.

At Dade Battlefield Memorial Park, John Hale was superintendent and extended to us every assistance. Later on, Lieutenant Alva Cook replaced him and continued with courtesy and helpfulness to aid our endeavors. Through countless visits in the park and the museum we have been grateful for the help of staff members Glenn Edwards and Paul McAllister.

The quest for information on Francis Langhorne Dade led the author to many people whom it has been a pleasure to know either personally or through correspondence. Particularly I want to name the following in Florida: Tom Brown of Frostproof; T. T. Wentworth of Pensacola; August Burghard of Nova University in Fort Lauderdale; William M. Dade of Miami; Miss Dorothy Dodd, Tallahassee; Harvey L. Wells in Clearwater; and Mrs. Blanche Coons of the DeLand Public Library. Out of the state there are John W. Dudley and Milton C. Russell of the Virginia State Library, Mrs. Virginia T. Saville of Richmond, and Mrs. G. M. Griffith of Baltimore.

Mrs. Leslie B. Lawton of Savannah, a descendant of Lieutenant Basinger's brother, gave the required access to the *Personal Reminiscences* which dealt with Lieutenant Basinger. Her son Edward Lawton of Connecticut also aided the research through many long and helpful letters. Also of vital help on Basinger were Mrs. Lilla M. Hawes of the Georgia Historical Society and Mrs. Christine Burroughs of the University Libraries in Athens, Georgia.

J. C. Billings of Kinston, North Carolina, was our

sole link with the hometown of Dr. Gatlin. Mr. Billings'
information and suggestions were invaluable.

In trying to discover the background and character of
the enlisted men who marched with Dade I was assisted
by strangers in many parts of the world who knew the
author only through letters of request and who searched
old records with generosity and concern. To mention them
all would be an endless task. Following is a partial list of
those who gave their time and knowledge that we might
meet the men in these pages: Mrs. Gladys Ladu of the
New York State Library who put me on the path of
Ransom Clarke's last resting place; Mrs. Marie C. Preston
of Geneseo, New York, found the cemetery records covering the Clarke plot and arranged for William Olmsted,
a student in Hamilton College, Clinton, New York, to
visit and photograph the grave on a bleak winter day.
Others in the United States were Kevin White of Boston;
Harold R. Manakee, Baltimore; Mrs. Amy Ver Nooy,
Poughkeepsie, New York; Mrs. Delia H. Pugh and John
W. Haines of Burlington, New Jersey; Marion R. Small,
Portland, Maine; Lois V. Given and R. N. Williams in
Philadelphia; Ferol O. Briggs, Jr., of Lynchburg, Virginia;
Pastor Bailey F. Davis of Amherst, Virginia; and Mrs.
Anne M. Miller, Hillsboro, North Carolina.

In Ireland help was given by M. C. Griffith of Dublin;
Patrick P. Devins of Sligo County; and E. Davison of
Belfast. I'm grateful to W. A. Thorburn of the Scottish
United Services Museum, an especially thoughtful and lit-
erate gentleman; Helen Armet of Edinburgh and George
MacBean and James Cameron of Inverness. Assistance was
rendered by Felise Hull of Maidstone, England.

In the broader fields I could not have secured half the
material used without the help of many staff members
of the New York Public Library, particularly Harold
Merklen and R. H. Carruthers. Virginia Daiker and Robert
H. Land in the Library of Congress produced obscure

letters and pictures. Colonel Raymond C. Ball of the Historical Services Division, Department of the Army, and George J. Stanfield of the National War College in Washington helped with military reference works.

From West Point I received immeasurable help and great encouragement from J. Thomas Russell, Frederick P. Todd, Colonel Thomas M. Metz, and Joseph M. O'Donnell.

Reconstructing the weather of one hundred and thirty years ago has been a challenge. Those who have helped meet it have been Al Duckworth, weather forecaster of Tampa; Keith Butson of Gainesville; Don Chamberlin, Clearwater; Barbara D. Simson of Yale University; and Gerald L. Barger and William H. Haggard of the Environmental Science Services Administration in Asheville, North Carolina.

The entire research project in relation to the Fort King Road would have been hopeless without the materials furnished by the Commissioner of Agriculture in Tallahassee, Doyle Conner, and C. F. Fuechsel in Arlington, Virginia, engineer with the United States Geological Survey.

The incredible resources of the National Archives and Record Service in Washington have been opened to my research by Victor Gondos, Jr., Elmer Parker, Elbert Huber, Garry D. Ryan, Edward J. Reese, Forest L. Williams, and John E. Taylor.

Varied and valuable help has been gratefully received from W. E. Rachels, W. R. Moore, Floyd Bradley, and Edwin C. Schafer of the Seaboard Air Line Railroad; Margaret Ruckert of the New Orleans Public Library; Laura Johnston of the St. Petersburg Public Library; Dr. Charleton W. Tebeau, University of Miami; Betty Bruce, Monroe County Public Library in Key West; the editors of the Richmond *Times Dispatch* and the Richmond *News Leader* who published my letters requesting information on Francis Dade; Graham P. Stansbury of St. Petersburg; and John E. Bibb of the National Guard Association of the United States.

I am grateful to the Board of Managers of the University of Florida Press who gave the final encomium—they agreed to publish the book.

I wish to thank my father and mother, Major and Mrs. William F. Laumer, for uncounted hours of assistance and encouragement since the 4th of March, 1927—all of which, one way and another, have resulted in this book.

And finally I welcome the opportunity to thank (however inadequate the word) my beloved wife Lois without whose steadfast love I would have accomplished little these past twenty-one years.

CONTENTS

Illustrations follow page 172

INTRODUCTION

CHANGE has so altered the face of Florida that it is difficult
to realize that there was a time when its interior was
deemed inaccessible; difficult to picture the day—little more
than a hundred years ago—when this smiling land was a
battlefield. But beneath the tropical patina of sunshine and
flowers lie the weapons of a forgotten war and the bones of
forgotten men. Where broad highways now wrap the state
with concrete, tenuous trails were once flattened by Indians'
moccasins and soldiers' boots. The dark river waters that
now sustain pleasure boats have known far longer the dugout of the Seminole and the log raft of the trooper. In parks
where tourists now scatter trash, white men and red once
fought and died.

The Florida War was "the longest, costliest and bloodiest
Indian war in United States history" spanning almost seven
years and costing the government thirty million dollars.
Before the end more than fifteen hundred soldiers were
dead[1] and all but three hundred of the surviving Indians
traveled the Trail of Tears to far Oklahoma.[2]

1. Holman Hamilton, *Zachary Taylor: Soldier of the Republic* (Indianap-
olis, Bobbs-Merrill Co., 1941), p. 122; *Record of Officers and Soldiers Killed in
Battle and Died in Service During the Florida War* (Washington, Government
Printing Office, 1882), p. 9.
2. Edwin C. McReynolds, *The Seminoles* (Norman, University of Oklahoma
Press, 1957), pp. 144, 151-242; *Record of Officers*, p. 9; Dale Van Every, *Disin-
herited: The Lost Birthright of the American Indian* (New York, William
Morrow & Co., 1966), p. 251. Mr. Van Every refers to the Trail of Tears as being

The issue was never really in doubt, for the relentless push of civilized man could be stayed but not stopped. The people living on the fringe of this greener pasture would never obey the strictures of their own laws or the threats of the savage owners but continued to push mile by mile and fence by fence until they reached the sea. This land was destined to be taken by the white men simply because it was here, though the Devil take the foremost. Forbidden by the government to encroach on the forests and hammocks retained by the Indians, the settlers still edged on, not unaware or (in some cases) unashamed of the illegality of their action, but urged on by a drive as irresistible as that of the lemming for the sea. And as surely as these pioneers were set upon, the call went out for soldiers to maintain the uneasy peace, broken, technically, by the Indians whose ever-shrinking acres the settlers were poaching upon.

To maintain peace, the government built nearly two hundred forts throughout the Territory of Florida, cleared three thousand miles of road through unexplored wilderness,[3] and sent over forty thousand men[4] into sporadic jungle warfare against a total of seven thousand men, women, and children of the Seminole Nation.[5]

Halfway down the west coast of Florida at Tampa Bay stood Fort Brooke, main debarkation point for incoming troops. One hundred and six miles north by the military road lay Fort King, an important military post and trading station. In December, 1835, one hundred and eight men led by Major Francis Langhorne Dade set out on this road. This is the story of those men.

---

a Cherokee term but in a real sense it surely applies as well to the tragic deportation of the Seminoles who, he says: "suffered so much more than other migrants before their start, [and] continued to suffer more en route."

3. Captain John MacKay and Lieutenant J. E. Blake, *Map of the Seat of War in Florida,* 1840, published by order of the Senate of the United States for the *Army and Navy Chronicle.*

4. Francis B. Heitman, *Historical Register and Dictionary of the United States Army* (Washington, Government Printing Office, 1903), II, 281.

5. *Record of Officers,* p. 9. While there is no certainty as to the exact population of the Seminole nation, this figure seems a likely estimate.

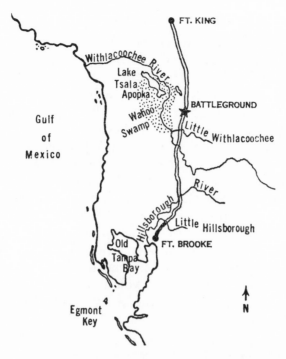

THE FIRST DAY

Wednesday, December 23, 1835

A HELL of a way to spend Christmas. Here it was the twenty-third and in two days they'd be part way to Fort King, squatting in a pine barren and hoping they could keep their scalps till New Year's.[1] Private Ransom

1. In the records of this history, as in all others, there are many conflicting reports, even (or perhaps, particularly) on such basic points as the dates upon which specific events occurred. In his official report on the fate of Major Dade and his command (Francis S. Belton to Adjutant General R. Jones, January 1, 1836), Captain Belton, in command at Fort Brooke, gave the date of departure as December 24, while Lieutenant George A. McCall states that they marched on December 25 (Major George A. McCall, *Letters from the Frontiers* [Philadelphia, 1868], p. 299). The author has relied, in this case, on Lieutenant John C. Casey (Casey to Thomas Basinger, January 2, 1836), quoted in "The Personal Reminiscences of William Starr Basinger, 1827-1910," a manuscript in the University of Georgia Library, written by a nephew of Lieutenant Basinger. Each writer is backed on his own date by other writers.

1

Clarke,[2] standing at ease in the right file, waited to move out. He could hear Charlie Heck, the drummer, as he continued to beat assembly while men tumbled out of the long barracks lining the company street to take their places in formation. Early in the morning like this you could see down past the officers' quarters, the flag pole, beyond the little schooner *Motto*,[3] and clear across Tampa Bay. Up ahead Clarke could see and hear big Sergeant Philip Cooper bellow above the muted talk of a hundred men as he formed them into two companies. Sergeant Cooper was German—tall, blond, and blue-eyed—and a professional soldier for the better part of his forty-two years. At the rear of the column the team of oxen hitched to the iron six-pounder waited silently with heads bowed while the company officers, handsome Lieutenant William Elon Basinger[4] and young Richard Henderson,[5] strode back and forth along the files giving authority to the commands of the sergeants.[6]

2. The names and spelling are taken from "Registers of Enlistments in the United States Army, 1798-1914" (Microcopy M233, roll 19, January, 1828-1835, and roll 20, 1835-39), National Archives (hereafter called "Enlistment Registers"). These registers were compiled from the many separate enlistment registers being kept in the various cities where recruiting offices were open from time to time. It should be safe to assume that these records are correct, at least to the extent that the recruit was in possession of the correct spelling of his name and the place of his birth. Other sources on Clarke were: "Enlistment Registers" (roll 19, 1833, p. 39, no. 162); Ransom Clarke, *The Surprising Adventures of Ransom Clarke Among the Indians in Florida* (Binghamton, N.Y., J. R. Orton, 1839); and the Clarke file from the National Archives and Records Service in Washington (hereafter referred to as N.A.R.S.).

The author has a typescript and tape recording of Clarke's work. An original copy of the pamphlet is in the possession of Mark Boyd in Tallahassee.

3. The *Motto* is variously described as a schooner and as a sloop, the technical difference being (prior to 1840) that a schooner carried two masts while a sloop had one. The commoner reference has been the former and we have accepted that term here.

4. The first sources for information on Lieutenant Basinger, as well as the other officers of the command, were Heitman, and George W. Cullum, *Biographical Register of Graduates and Former Cadets of the United States Military Academy* (West Point, N.Y., West Point Alumni Foundation, Inc., 1960), but other sources provided much greater depth. In the case of Lieutenant Basinger, the most helpful was "Personal Reminiscences."

5. Other than Heitman and sources of simple statistics, information on Lieutenant Henderson was found in the records supplied by the N.A.R.S.

6. It should be made clear that with the exception of Dade and Captain Upton S. Fraser, we have found no specific mention of officers being mounted.

Ransom Clarke had been standing formations for two years now, ever since he'd joined up back in Rochester, New York, but this one was different. Lately he had been the regular mail carrier for the army on the Fort Brooke-Fort King run and he knew that the mood of the Seminoles was ominous. There had already been trouble and it wasn't over yet. Clarke had characteristics that made for a good soldier: courage, resourcefulness, and determination, typified by his escape just a year ago from a capsized boat in Mobile Bay while the remainder of the crew were lost.[7] He was twenty-three, of medium height, with a swarthy complexion, hazel eyes, and a strong instinct for survival. He put his faith in brains and guts and he didn't count on much luck.

Lieutenant Basinger of Savannah was in command of C Company, Second Artillery Regiment, since Captain Gardiner[8] had been given command of the entire detachment. Basinger was just two years older than Private Clarke and admired by officers and men alike. He had completed four years at West Point without a single demerit, attaining the rank of cadet sergeant-major under the Cadet Adjutant, Robert E. Lee, and when Lee graduated in 1829 Basinger had succeeded him as adjutant, graduating second in his class. He excelled in everything he did and to the eyes of Clarke and the other men of his company he presented an appearance of strength and firm good looks. His short black

Our assumptions in this connection are based upon a notation for December, 1835, in the Fort Brooke Post Returns (Microcopy 617, 1824-40, roll 147, N.A.R.S.) which states: "Battle . . . fought . . . 8 horses killed." At the time of battle, as will be shown, it seems likely that four horses were in harness to the cannon leaving four others as mounts. It appears reasonable that the four ranking officers would have employed them.

7. A late staff officer [Woodburne Potter], *The War in Florida: Being an Exposition of Its Causes, and an Accurate History of the Campaigns of Generals Clinch, Gaines, and Scott* (Baltimore, Md., Lewis & Coleman, 1836), p. 107; Clarke, *Surprising Adventures*, p. 107.

8. Statistical information on Captain Gardiner was taken from Heitman and Cullum. Again, the Gardiner file in the N.A.R.S. made available letters, pension claims, and so forth. Additional descriptions have been taken from John Bemrose, *Reminiscences of the Second Seminole War*, ed. John K. Mahon (Gainesville, University of Florida Press, 1966), p. 64.

beard made him look older than he was, but the scarlet sash
and golden epaulettes gave the proper dash of youth.[9] A
friend described him as "all that an ingenuous mind could
imagine for a youthful soldier. Frank, brave, warm-hearted,
and yet gay, with . . . the lurkings about him yet of boy-
hood. . . ."[10] Perhaps he inspired more confidence than he
felt, but the men would never know it. He had written to
his mother two weeks before relating how all efforts had
been turned toward strengthening the fort and erecting
further defenses against the Indians "who are in a state of
hostility and from whom we are every day expecting an
attack. But everything is now finished and . . . all the
Indians in Florida could not do us the slightest injury."[11]
Maybe this was a little over-optimistic—even for the company remaining in Fort Brooke—but Lieutenant Basinger
wasn't worried. Shortly the gates would swing open and he
and the rest of the detachment of one hundred men and
eight officers would march out, straight through the Indian
nation. And even if he *were* worried, orders were orders.

Brevet Second Lieutenant Richard Henderson, second in
command of Company C, was a young man who had received
his commission at the military academy less than six months
before. Since the age of fourteen he had dutifully prepared
for a military career and had graduated from West Point in
the top quarter of his class. Now he was nineteen with six
years given to his father's wishes, but that was enough. There
were other professions more attractive than the military for
a young man of education and high hopes. He had applied
to the President for discharge and an end to this service

9. This and most of the following descriptive material on the uniforms has
been gathered from uniform regulations of the period supplied by the N.A.R.S.,
specifically: Article 65 of 1825—Uniform and Dress of the Army, paragraphs 321,
822-88; Article 52 of 1836—Uniform and Dress of the Army; the following
orders from the Adjutant General's Office—No. 36 (May 23, 1829), No. 50 (June
11, 1832), No. 89 (October 13, 1832), No. 10 (February 8, 1833), No. 38 (May 2,
1833), and No. 36 (1839). In addition, a fine series of paintings by H. A. Ogden,
"Uniforms of the United States Army," Groups 4 and 5, were studied.

10. "Personal Reminiscences," p. 81.

11. Lieutenant Basinger to Mrs. Peter Basinger, December 10, 1835, in
"Personal Reminiscences," Appendix II.

on a bleak frontier. Ironically, acceptance of the resignation had come only two days ago[12] on the schooner carrying the reinforcements that simultaneously presented him with an opportunity for action and adventure. But only he and Captain Francis Smith Belton, Commandant of Fort Brooke since the eleventh of the month,[13] knew that he was technically a civilian now, and the resignation could be ignored while danger threatened. He'd make this trip through the hostile nation and have a story to tell when he got back to Jackson, Tennessee.

Within the twelve-foot split-log palisade walls[14] the troops stood in double file, a composite of many outfits but standing now as Company C, Second Artillery, and Company B, Third Artillery, forty-nine soldiers and noncommissioned officers in one unit, fifty in the other. The noise and activity that had enveloped the fort since before sunrise at eight minutes to seven was slowly settling.[15] By the walls of the 260-foot barracks stood a few unattached troopers exchanging derisive, low-voiced comments with the men in ranks. From a window of a heavy-timbered blockhouse pretty Frances Kyle Basinger watched her husband of two years as he stood at the head of his company. His repeated assurance of confidence had been delivered in such good spirits that she had tried, not altogether successfully, to banish her fears. He had assured her that he would be back "in a couple of weeks at the farthest," and now there was nothing to do except wave goodby when he passed and then count the hours until his return.[16]

12. Benjamin Alvord, *An Address Before the Dialectic Society of the Corps of Cadets at West Point* (New York, Wiley and Putnam, 1839), p. 40.

13. Belton to Jones, December 12, 1835, in *The Territorial Papers of the United States*, ed. Clarence Edwin Carter (Washington, Government Printing Office, 1956-62), XXIV, 949. Volumes XXII-XXVI constitute the *Florida Territorial Papers*, and will hereafter be referred to as *FTP*.

14. McCall, p. 133.

15. *America Nautical Almanac* for 1959, quoted by Mark M. Boatner III, *The Civil War Dictionary* (New York, David McKay Company, Inc., 1959), pp. 820-21.

16. Mrs. William Basinger to Mrs. Peter Basinger, March 12, 1836, in "Personal Reminiscences," Appendix VI.

The column stretched for some seventy yards from the drooping cannon muzzle at the rear to Captain George Washington Gardiner at the head.[17] As senior officer he was in charge of the entire detachment; eight officers,[18] ninety-nine men,[19] four oxen in harness to the cannon, and a single horse hitched to a light wagon carrying ten days' provisions.[20] George Gardiner was so short he looked stunted, "being almost as thick as he was long, and not standing much higher than five feet . . .";[21] but since his graduation from West Point in 1814 the little captain had served in many posts—through the War of 1812 and as instructor of infantry tactics and artillery at the Point— and this hike through a hundred miles of enemy territory might not be any worse than similar service in the Cherokee Nation back in 1830. And when General Clinch sent down an order for reinforcements for Fort King, it didn't pay to sit around.

Gardiner shifted in his saddle. In the blockhouse his wife Frances lay deathly ill. She might be dead before he returned from this assignment, but there was nothing he could do for her that the assistant surgeon of the post, Dr. H. L. Heiskell,[22] had not already done. This man's army guaranteed your pay and bacon, but the health of your family was

17. Belton to Adjutant General R. Jones, March 25, 1836; McCall, p. 300; Alvord address, p. 40.

18. The roster of officers is given in "The Men of Dade's Command," pp. 177-80 below, as listed by Captain Belton in his official report to Adjutant General R. Jones, January 1, 1836, and again March 25, 1836, N.A.R.S.

19. This number is taken from the "Enlistment Registers," where the notation "Killed by Indians at Dade's Massacre in Florida" followed the name of each man, with the exception of the survivors. In one source (Potter), reference is made to an unnamed servant accompanying the command, but he is not mentioned by any one of the Fort Brooke observers who wrote of the departure, and since the circumstances of the march were hardly conducive to the inclusion of servants, this has been assumed to be incorrect.

20. It has commonly been assumed that the Negro interpreter Louis Pacheco left the fort with the command. However, records recently discovered indicate that he left later in the day. See note 85, below.

21. Bemrose, p. 64.

22. H. L. Heiskell to Surgeon General J. Lovell, January 9, 1836. The text of this letter indicates that Dr. Heiskell was the senior medical officer at Fort Brooke during this period.

up to God. At least the children were safe with Frances' father in Key West.[23] He wished she were there too.

Behind him eighty-eight artillerymen in two companies shouldered the unaccustomed black leather straps of eight-pound, five-foot muskets, their bayonets pointing at the huge live-oak limbs that formed a canopy sixty feet above their heads. Spanish moss, like great gray icicles in the cold blue morning, pointed back. If trouble came a man could use a musket, the sergeant had said, even if he was artillery. Over their dark blue double-breasted cloth coats the white cross-belts made a startling contrast. A double row of gilt eagle buttons four inches apart ran from the collar to the hem, three and a half inches above the knees. The stiff standing collar, two inches high with the red-bound edging of the artillery corps, kept a man's head up by necessity. Below the coat, plain sky-blue trousers reached down over low black boots. Outside their coats each man wore a two-inch wide white leather belt held in the front with a plain round buckle. Short on the gear of regular infantry, these eighty-eight carried their cartridges in hand-made pouches tied to their belts.[24] Not too military and not too handy for a man in a hurry, but with luck they wouldn't need them.

Scattered through the ranks were eleven men on detached service from Company B, Fourth Infantry, a part of the reinforcements that had come in aboard the *Motto* from Key West only two days before.[25] Except for the white collar trim instead of red and a little more ease with a musket they looked just like the rest, just like soldiers everywhere— underpaid, overworked, and ready for a change.

There was Private Alpheas Gillet, just nineteen years

23. Potter, p. 103.

24. Cynthia K. Farr, *Tampa's Earliest Living Pioneer: A Sketch From the Life of Mrs. Nancy Jackson* (Tallahassee, c. 1900), p. 11. This little pamphlet was taken from the reminiscences of Nancy Collar Jackson (as related to Farr by Jackson) around the turn of the century when Mrs. Jackson was over eighty. Many details related by Mrs. Jackson after the lapse of more than sixty years are in error, but there is little reason to doubt that the basic event, here related, is in error, since she participated.

25. Belton to Jones, January 1, 1836.

old, from New York State, signed up for three years. In
another eighteen months he'd be back home in Troy and
able to tell the folks about his adventures on the frontier
in Florida.[26] And Aaron Jewell, artilleryman in Company C
with Gillet, a farmer from Vermont, tired of plowing rocky
hillsides but unused to Florida winters. For twenty-four
years he'd seen snow for six out of every twelve months, but
here the sun was blazing over the barrack's roof bright and
clear and his greatcoat was stored in the knapsack riding
across his shoulders.[27] And Joseph Sprague, another ex-
farmer from Vermont, with brown hair and calloused hands
waited in the morning's chill.[28]

The drummer shifted to the long roll warning the lag-
gards to fall in. Sergeants Cooper and Vailing, both German
and both professionals, at a sign from their commanders
silenced their companies with the abruptness of which only
sergeants are capable and swung about ready to move out.
Their red stripe of rank an inch and a half wide ran from
hip to ankle and the slash sleeves of their coats ended in
cuffs with three buttons and embroidered loops called
Austrian Knots, a symbol of rank that dated from the
Middle Ages. The new "Roman Pattern" short swords hung
below the left hip, the scabbard suspended from the leather
belt by a hook, the belt itself clasped by an S-hook con-
necting two bronze discs, the left bearing crossed cannons,
the other an eagle. In the expectant silence the men could
hear the brisk shuffle of the officers' mounts as they faced
the front; from the bay the shrill cry of gulls drifted across
the compound.

An officer who had been in earnest conversation with
Captain Belton near the commandant's office suddenly
swung into his saddle, silver infantry spurs flashing briefly
in the morning sun. Horse and rider crossed to the head of
the column that waited on the verge of motion. Captain

26. "Enlistment Registers" (roll 19, 1834, p. 77, no. 103).
27. "Enlistment Registers" (roll 19, 1834, p. 100, no. 67).
28. "Enlistment Registers" (roll 19, 1834, p. 180, no. 185).

Gardiner turned in his saddle to take a salute, while Lieutenant Benjamin Alvord and young Dr. John Slade Gatlin watched in silence.

Brevet Major Francis Langhorne Dade enjoyed an audience and he had an appreciative one here. It was typical that in that one moment when the men stood steady and quiet waiting for the command to march he would come from the wings to stage center.

Major Dade was forty-three years old and the very model of Virginia chivalry. A descendent of the Francis Dade who had settled back in 1645 on the hills overlooking the valley of the Potomac, he had been born on February 22, 1792, in King George County, to a heritage of military prowess that he considered himself able and proud to uphold.[29] With the attention of the entire fort, Dade apologized for the unseemly interruption and verified the condition of Gardiner's wife. He made clear his respect for the captain's devotion to duty but would he perhaps allow the major to offer himself as a substitute in this tedious business in order for the captain to remain with his lady? The women of the post were unanimous in feeling that her husband's presence was critical to Mrs. Gardiner's recovery while the major had no ties here and would as soon be on the road. If the captain would agree, the major would be most honored.

Gardiner, deeply concerned over his wife's condition but averse by training to backing out of an assignment, especially

29. Sources on Francis Langhorne Dade are surprisingly brief and have been found in the following: Heitman, p. 350; the Alderman Library at the University of Virginia (a notebook containing genealogical data on Dade and other related families); *Appleton's Dictionary of American Biography*, II, 53; *The National Cyclopedia of American Biography*, XII, 196-97; *Harper's Encyclopedia of United States History*, III, 2; Horace Edwin Hayden, *Virginia Genealogies*, pp. 731-33; *The Virginia Magazine of History and Biography*, XX, 210-12, 323-29; *William and Mary College Quarterly*, XII, 245-50; H. Ragland Eubank, *The Authentic Guide Book of the Historic Neck of Virginia* (1934), pp. 25-27; *Homes and Gardens in Old Virginia*, ed. Frances Archer Christian and Suzanne Williams Massie (Richmond, Virginia, Garrett & Massie, Inc., 1939), pp. 3-4, 310-12; and the genealogical column of the Richmond *Times Dispatch*, March 6, 1910. For a man who came from a family of not inconsiderable prominence and position and whose death was mourned nationally, Francis Dade seems to have been forgotten except by the compilers of out-of-date encyclopedias.

when it appeared that the assignment would face trouble, hesitated, but Dade's argument was logical and persuasive and he reluctantly agreed. With another exchange of salutes, the captain turned over his command to Major Dade and with a tug on the reins wheeled his horse toward the block house and his wife.[30]

At a signal from Dade the three mounted officers quickly turned out of the ranks and trotted smartly toward the little civilian group standing near the gate in the north wall. Reining in, Dade spoke to them on behalf of the officers and men, reassuring them as to the safety of the command and expressing gratitude for their good wishes. Sitting his horse with perfect poise, one white-gloved hand lightly holding the reins just over the pommel of his polished saddle, the major exuded the glamour of a man of destiny. His natural good looks were enhanced by the cut of his uniform, from the silver epaulettes on his broad shoulders to the knee-high black leather boots that rested in silver stirrups. His black beard lay against the dark blue of his greatcoat and the stock of his favorite double-barrelled shotgun projected from the rifle boot slung to his saddle.[31] His great curved cavalry saber hung below his left hip, the gleaming silver grip matching the embroidered silver horn on the skirt of his coat. His words were well spoken and sincere—Sir Galahad seemed to look from the brave and level eyes—then with a smile and a casual salute, he wheeled and with his officers, spurred on.[32]

"Fo-whad, ho-oo-oo"—before the command faded, the column was in motion. Executing the saber salute with a flourish, Major Dade led his adopted command past Captain Belton and through the gate where pretty Nancy Collar stood watching with her younger sister. The two of them with their mother and the Reverend Mr. Simmon's wife had been up all night making the powder bags that the passing artillerymen carried on their belts.[33]

30. Alvord, p. 40; McCall, p. 300; Belton to Jones, March 25, 1836.
31. Thomas Jesup to Colonel John B. Dade, December 16, 1842.
32. Farr, p. 11.   33. Ibid.

Captain Belton stood apart from the civilian group inside the palisade. He was uneasy, and Dade's words from the evening before ran through his mind as he stood with his staff officers and took the salute. He and Dade had been returning from the camp of friendly Indians across the river, discussing the risk and possible danger in the proposed march. They had paused just by the doorway of the surgeon's quarters when he had told Dade emphatically that before *he* would have accepted the assignment that Gardiner had taken—to face what he considered certain death for himself and his men—he would resign his commission. And Major Dade had disagreed just as emphatically, had said that if the command had devolved upon him he, like Gardiner, would have accepted it. Rather than be called a coward, he would die first.[34] And now his noble act had placed him in command, erect and handsome in the saddle and with every look of confidence. God grant that it wasn't misplaced.

Beyond the gate stretched a wide and barren patch of white sand from which the natural growth of palmettos had long since been cleared to guard against the stealthy approach of Indians. The heavy stand of yellow pine trees that had once covered the land had been sawed into lumber through the years, first for the men's barracks in 1824 and subsequently for officers' quarters, the guardhouse, storehouses, two blockhouses, a powder magazine, the wharf, and the stables.[35] Of the original growth only the gray oaks still stood,[36] sheltering the little huddle of log buildings and spreading out over the surrounding acres of sand. To the left the Hillsborough River flowed past the fort and into Tampa Bay giving the camp a water boundary on two sides. On the right, swamps and marshland filled the interval between land and sea. Standing fifteen feet above the water

34. *Ibid.*
35. Dr. James W. Covington, "Life at Fort Brooke, 1824-1836," *Florida Historical Quarterly* (hereafter *FHQ*), XXXVI (April, 1958), 319-30; *Army and Navy Chronicle* (B. Homans, editor), II (January-June, 1836), 79.
36. McCall, p. 133.

and surrounded by a dry moat eight feet deep,[37] the fort commanded both the bay and the only land approach which rose gently toward the northeast.

North of the fort and strung along the east shore of the river were the conglomerate shelters of assorted pioneers. Previously huddled in rude shacks directly under the protective walls of Fort Brooke, they had edged cautiously out over the years, planting one store and then another until now more than a dozen lined the river bank. There were no more than 100 civilians and they were here against all the rules of the country, including that of common sense. Allowed to stay only by the sufferance of the military, these people were the very essence of the nation's conflict with the Indians. Quartered now within the walls of the fort and with their buildings boarded, most of them stood around the gate and watched with mixed feelings as the soldiers passed.

Augustus Steel, Connecticut entrepreneur, had been in the territory for ten years doing one thing and another; now he was the first county judge, having authority over the five million acres of wilderness that had recently been set aside as Hillsborough County.[38] As postmaster, he knew most of the men and had occasionally read their letters to them—he knew, too, those who got no letters.

Bill Saunders, from Alabama, had been living near the fort for seven years; earlier he had run the first general store on Florida's west coast.[39] Levi Collar, first white American settler in the vicinity and father of twenty-year-old Nancy, made a good living by supplying the garrison with vegetables that he raised across the river near his cabin.[40]

These men and others like them would always be in places

37. Alexander Beaufort Meek, *Journal of the Florida Expedition*, quoted by Rembert W. Patrick in *Aristocrat in Uniform: General Duncan L. Clinch* (Gainesville, University of Florida Press, 1963), p. 63.

38. *FTP*, XXIV, 949; William Worth to the Adjutant General, May 12, 1845, *FTP*, XXVI, 1073.

39. Karl H. Grismer, *Tampa: A History of the City of Tampa and the Tampa Bay Region of Florida* (St. Petersburg, Florida, 1950), p. 65.

40. Grismer, p. 61.

like this, on the frontiers that white men had to have. They represented something basic in the makeup of Americans: the desire for space around them and for freedom. Back home in Massachusetts, or Tennessee, society would begin to settle its restrictive coils about men like them, and then one day they'd just be gone. And if you watched, sooner or later they'd show up around places like Fort Smith, Arkansas, or here at Fort Brooke, in Florida—anyplace where a man could just move in and with a few tools put up something to live in and start scratching in the ground for a little garden, keep a couple of chickens, and trade whatever he knew how to make to others, driven here by the same instinct. They wouldn't be too constrained by the niceties of law, and yet in a pinch, without any speeches, they'd be pretty likely to risk what little they had, including life, to help a neighbor or even a stranger. They lived hard and worked hard, and usually they wore out and died pretty early. Racial supremacy was their heritage and they didn't wonder much about the rights of red men or black. They were too busy clearing and planting and building to concern themselves with the opinions of savages who lived in the forests, perfectly willing to ignore them while putting the earth to what they considered its proper use. True, sometimes here in Florida, as on the other frontiers, the shadowy people of the wild would actively resist the steady push of white pioneers and then there was bound to be trouble; but that was the soldier's job, and they'd better be about it.

The major led the column across the soft, cold sand where the Fort King Road[41] wound between the sturdy oaks,

41. Research to determine the exact course of the Fort King Road began with the original government survey maps of Florida which were begun in 1840. Previous research (see Frank Laumer, "The Ft. Dade Site," *The Florida Anthropologist*, XVI [June, 1963], 33-42) has shown that these township plats, together with the field notes, gave the exact point at which the Fort King Road crossed each section line and a close approximation of the road's course from each section line to the next. By obtaining each township plat (and the field notes pertaining to it) through which the road passed, we were able to make up a composite showing the entire route from Fort Brooke to the battleground, sixty miles north. We next obtained a modern set of maps (United States Geological Survey, Washington, D.C., 1943-60) covering the same townships, which in

passing the log stores along the river and the orderly grove of five hundred orange trees[42] set out when the fort was new and now drooping under the weight of their winter fruit. They crossed the great circle of beaten sand where, in less anxious times, Dade had raced his favorite mare Richard the Third in the first Derby held in Florida and had lost.[43] The screech of the three-foot wooden wheels turning on the iron axle of the gun carriage rose in the morning air as an accompaniment to the heavy drumming of marching feet. Long after the men were gone from sight to the north, the sound of their passage could still be heard by the silent watchers at the gate.

So Major Francis Dade and his little command were on their way, sabers gleaming and emblems winking cheerfully in the sunlight. They thought their destination was Fort King and their path the Fort King Road, but they were wrong. A different destiny had been determined by the bronzed and silent men who watched them from the shadows of the wood, and the path they took was really the road to war.

It was three years now since Colonel James Gadsden, acting for the Secretary of War, had managed to get a group

this series included the following quadrangles: Tampa, Thonotosassa, Antioch, Sulphur Springs, Zephyrhills, Dade City, Lacoochee, St. Catherine, Bushnell, and Wahoo. Using the specifications of the original survey, we superimposed the Fort King Road on these maps (see William M. Goza, "The Ft. King Road—1963," *FHQ*, XLIII [July, 1964], 52-70). Consistently, we found that each bend and turn in the old maps which passed a lake or swamp or hilltop was matched perfectly on the more recent survey. Field trips to spot-check various locations revealed time and again that the actual path of the old road still existed. In addition, a study of various aerial survey photographs showed the road winding like a dark thread across the modern countryside, matching the early survey curve for curve. In order to familiarize ourselves with the route traveled by Dade's command, a small group began from Tampa and walked the entire route to the battleground in December, 1963. We camped each night on the site of Dade's bivouac, or as close to it as our research to that date made possible. (Subsequent work has indicated that we missed the site only once—Dade's camp on the fourth night.) Through copious notes taken, many details of Dade's march have, we believe, been made historically correct.

42. McCall, p. 199-200.

43. Pensacola *Gazette*, April 15, 1826, quoted by D. B. McKay in *Pioneer Florida*, I (Tampa, The Southern Publishing Company, 1959), 15.

of Seminole Indian leaders to sign a conditional piece of diplomatic expediency called the Treaty of Payne's Landing, on the Oklawaha River. On the ninth day of May, 1832, by the swiftly flowing water, chiefs Jumper, Micanopy, Alligator, and others had put their marks on the white man's paper. While sunlight filled the clearing and flowers nodded, the dusky men with egret feathers in their hair signed away their land for the white man's promise. They would be given (they were told) a portion of land beyond the sunset called Arkansas, they would be taken there and given clothing and tools and, in addition, the White Father would give them some sixty thousand dollars over a period of fifteen years.[44]

Doomed as much by native human honesty and trust as by their lack of weapons and organization, the signing chiefs in this instance, as in so many others, could not possibly have understood either the exact words of the treaty or its implications. They had to depend for translation of the document on Negroes adopted by the tribe, Negroes whose knowledge of English had been gained while in slavery on southern farms, and who had picked up an even poorer comprehension of the Seminole dialect. With an army officer reading the formal wording of a government document to an ignorant Negro to be translated by him into Seminole, it was unlikely that the words of the White Father in Washington were correctly understood by the assorted chiefs who made their marks of acquiescence. But even if they had had the gift of tongues they would not have been able to comprehend, for they were red and these hard-eyed men were white. The Indian could have all the meanness of a grown child,

44. *Indian Affairs, Laws, and Treaties*, ed. Charles J. Kappler (Washington, 1904), II, 398-400; John Lee Williams, *The Territory of Florida* (New York, A. T. Goodrich, 1837; reprinted in the Floridian Facsimile and Reprint Series, Gainesville, University of Florida Press, 1962), p. 236; Myer M. Cohen, *Notices of Florida and the Campaigns* (Charleston, S.C., Burges & Honour, 1836; reprinted in the Floridian Facsimile and Reprint Series, Gainesville, University of Florida Press, 1964), pp. 51-52; McCall, p. 301; Joshua R. Giddings, *The Exiles of Florida* (Columbus, Ohio, Follett, Foster & Company, 1858; reprinted in the Floridian Facsimile and Reprint Series, Gainesville, University of Florida Press, 1964), pp. 82-83.

the petulance of thwarted desires, and the passion to kill in
retribution, but only the white men possessed a heritage
of irresistible acquisition. The Indian would rise, hunt, and
sleep, but the soldiers in dusty blue never slept, and somehow with every sunrise the hunting land grew smaller.

Now, finally, the white men would have it all. One-third
of the Seminoles were to leave Florida as early as possible
during 1833, another third in 1834, and the remainder
in 1835. Discouraged by crop failure which they took to be
a sign from the gods (and perhaps overawed by the threats
of Colonel Gadsden, acting for the government), fifteen
chiefs finally signed the conditional agreement. Twenty
years of attrition since their first clash with American
troops in 1812[45] had taken their toll, and since that time
the Seminole efforts at appeasement had brought them to
this. They had only one legal tract of land left in the
interior of the state and the ravenous land-appetite of the
white men would soon take that. It was not quality land
—even Governor William P. DuVal admitted that this
reservation allowed the Seminoles by the Moultrie Creek
Treaty was "by far the poorest and most miserable region
I ever beheld."[46] But white misfits, good and bad, had
swarmed into the new land acquired then, and now stood
panting on the edges of this last reserve. Gradually the
Seminoles were beginning to comprehend the white man's
ways. When urged by DuVal to lead his people to the new
treaty land, Chief Neamathla had replied: "Do you think
. . . that I can see nothing of what is going on around
me? Ever since I was a small boy I have seen the white
people steadily encroaching upon the Indians, and driving
them from their homes and hunting grounds. When I was
a boy, the Indians still roamed undisputed over the country
lying between the Tennessee River and the great Sea [Gulf

45. Edwin C. McReynolds, *The Seminoles,* pp. 48-49; Irvin M. Peithmann,
The Unconquered Seminole Indians (St. Petersburg, Fla., Great Outdoors Association, 1957), p. 15.
46. Governor William P. DuVal to Thomas L. McKenney, February 22, 1826,
FTP, XXIII, 445-48; Peithmann, p. 21.

of Mexico] of the South, and now, where there is nothing left them but the hunting grounds in Florida, the white men covet that. I will tell you plainly, if I had the power, I would cut the throat of every white man in Florida."[47] Governor DuVal, with the inalienable right of power, peremptorily removed him.[48]

For eight years there had technically been peace. Actually, the harassment never ended. White men, especially slave hunters, could see no wall around the Seminole lands until an Indian tried to leave. With the permission of the Secretary of War,[49] whites could travel throughout the reservation in search of runaway slaves and this easily became a *carte blanche* to apprehend *any* Negro, whether free or a slave of the Seminoles—and by what seemed to them only a slight extension of this policy they went on to kidnap from the reservation any Indian who had, or might have, Negro blood. The wages of appeasement were being exacted in full measure.

But the white men were always ready with a new treaty —and perhaps this time it would be different. At any rate the Indians had been granted the privilege of inspecting this new land west of the Mississippi to assure themselves that it really was beyond the grasp of the settlers and slave-hunters, that the game was plentiful, that *here* the red man could make a new beginning in a new land. And if the land was without promise, then they could still stay here in the land of flowers where a hundred years of their past lived in the forests and the hammocks. They would visit this Arkansas, then return to their people and let them make their choice.

In September, 1832, seven of the chiefs, including Jumper and Alligator, escorted by Major John Phagan, their agent,

47. Peithmann, p. 21.

48. McReynolds, p. 104; Mark F. Boyd, *Florida Aflame* (Florida Board of Parks and Historic Memorials, Tallahassee, 1951), pp. 45-46, portions of this were previously published in *FHQ*, XXX (July, 1951), under the title "The Seminole War: Its Background and Onset."

49. Giddings, p. 80; Peithmann, p. 22.

set out on the thousand-mile journey. By steamboat they crossed "the great sea of the south," docked at New Orleans and proceeded north by river steamer up the Mississippi and Arkansas rivers to the vicinity of Little Rock. From there they rode on horseback the final two hundred miles into the no man's land between Arkansas and Oklahoma called Indian Territory. Here the weakened remnants of the once great tribes of America were being systematically dumped: Cherokees, Choctaws, Chickasaws, Kiowas, Wichitas, Comanches, and the relatives of the Seminoles, the Creeks. In the shadow of the Ozarks lay a pleasant prairie between two branches of the Canadian River, a rectangle twenty miles by forty.[50] This was the slot set aside for seven thousand Seminoles—less than one-tenth the size of their reduced Florida reservation. With their agent and led by the guides provided by the army they explored this new country, its woods, waterholes, streams, and neighbors. Finally, on March 28, 1833, Major Phagan, the chiefs, and three commissioners of the United States government met at Fort Gibson, a 5,500-acre military reservation[51] northeast of the proposed Seminole reservation on the east bank of the Neosho River, commanded by Brigadier General Matthew Arbuckle.[52]

It was now six months since the Seminoles had left their homes. Major Phagan was a man of violent passions, and bitter arguments had changed the chiefs' attitude toward him from indifference to aversion. Now he brought out a document for them to sign, but allayed their concern for its contents by explaining that this was merely a certification that the "land was good."

Six months and a thousand miles are a long time and a

50. *The Columbian Atlas of the World We Live In* (New York, Hunt & Eaton, 1893), pp. 274-75.

51. *United States Military Reservations, National Cemeteries, and Military Parks* (Washington, Government Printing Office, 1916), pp. 307-8.

52. McCall, p. 301; McReynolds, pp. 123-24; DuVal to Lewis Cass, May 30, 1832, *FTP*, XXIV, 711; DuVal to John Robb, October 11, 1832, *FTP*, XXIV, 740-41.

long way for men who live intimately with nature. The Indian leaders had seen and heard enough and more of the white culture, they had taken note of the proximity of the hated Creeks who would share the proposed new land of the Seminoles. They wanted only to go home. Their understanding of the portent of the paper before them must be through the Negro Abraham, once a slave belonging to a Dr. Sierre of Pensacola; he had been given refuge by the Seminole people and had accompanied them to the Indian Territory as official Seminole interpreter. Like John Phagan, he assured them that the words were good. One by one, then, they signed: John Hicks, Holata Emathla, Jumper, Coa Hadjo, Charley Emathla (brother of Holata), Yahadjo, and Nehathoclo (representing Sam Jones).[53] And as each one stepped to the table, grasped the pen in awkward and unfamiliar fingers, and made his identifying mark, Abraham, the only voice between two worlds, watched with satisfaction. In his pocket was the white man's bribe for betrayal of his Seminole hosts.[54]

The stolid men in shabby cotton were a pathetic contrast to the starched, black-coated commissioners (Monfort Stokes, Henry L. Ellsworth, and the Reverend John Schermerhorn) and the government officers headed by General Arbuckle.

Two thousand years of civilization had produced clean, strong men with a heritage of honor, truth, and courage. In a log fort on this windswept frontier of that civilization they clasped hands with savages whose unclean bodies were covered by absurd costumes and whose heritage was as ephemeral as the wind. Yet trust and honor were this day wrapped in shabby cotton and dishonor wore a clean white shirt.

The delegation returned to Florida and there Major

53. This document, known as the Treaty of Fort Gibson, was signed on March 28, 1833.

54. McReynolds, p. 125; McCall, p. 301; Peithmann, pp. 22-23; Cohen, p. 53; Boyd, *Florida Aflame*, pp. 45-46.

Phagan was dismissed from government service for mis-
handling of funds. His successor as Indian agent was General
Wiley Thompson, a Virginian by birth, whose career had
been long and honorable in both military and political
fields. He had risen to the rank of major general in the
Georgia militia during the War of 1812 and had served
six terms in the House of Representatives from the state
of Georgia. He was a strong advocate of Indian removal,
but was prepared to be fair and reasonable with his charges
within his own frame of reference. At fifty-two he was lean,
gray-haired, and in poor health, but the demands of the
position should not be excessive and he hoped to spend
the coming years smoothing the way for implementation
of government policy while bringing fair and Christian
treatment to the Seminoles.[55]

The Seminole Indian Agency was only one hundred
yards from the palisade surrounding Fort King while the
sutler's combined store and home was five hundred yards
farther to the northwest, set on a hill and backed against
a thick hammock of palmetto. In 1826, a year before the
establishment of Fort King, the agency had been built at
the northern terminus of the military road leading up
from Fort Brooke on Tampa Bay. The agency office was
a log building with a high roof and surrounding porches.[56]
When Thompson had arrived on a cold winter evening in
1833 to take possession as agent, he had found the agency
house with no lock on the door and occupied only by a
handyman named Dunlap. During the succeeding nine
months he had straightened out the few books left by his
predecessor, begun a little garden on the adjacent land,
and debated the practicality of sending for his family.[57]

Meanwhile the Seminole delegation had held meetings

55. McReynolds, p. 128; Daniel Kurtz to John Phagan, August 30, 1833,
FTP, XXIV, 876; Niles' Weekly Register, L (Baltimore, April 2, 1836), 83.
56. Rembert W. Patrick, Aristocrat in Uniform: General Duncan L.
Clinch (Gainesville, University of Florida Press, 1963), p. 98; Joseph W. Harris
to George Gibson, December 30, 1835, quoted in Boyd, Florida Aflame, p. 71.
57. Thompson to Cass, December 2, 1833, in FTP, XXIV, 916-18.

throughout the Nation telling their people that they had
traveled to the land beyond the Mississippi, that they
had signed a paper there at the insistence of their hosts
indicating that the land, as land, was "no doubt good,"[58]
but they did not want to take their people there. According
to the provisions of the Treaty of Payne's Landing they
must report to the agent the wishes of the Nation, but
they, the chiefs, had been to the Territory and they had
no wish to return. The people must consider it and when
they could speak with one voice, the chiefs would talk with
General Thompson and give him their decision.

The first meeting of the new agent and his charges was
arranged for Thursday, October 23, 1834, at the agency
office.[59] The porch of the long building was crowded with
Seminole warriors who had accompanied the chiefs to
the Great Council and with the wives of the chiefs, who
watched and listened through the open windows while
Seminole children played in the grass-grown sand of the
compound. In utter silence they stared at each man in
turn as he rose to speak. On one side of the council table
sat General Thompson and his staff headed by Major
William A. Graham with stout General Duncan Lamont
Clinch, in command of the United States forces in Florida,
in full dress uniform. Mr. David Levy, a gentleman of St.
Augustine,[60] would take notes of the proceedings. Across
from them were the assembled chiefs, stolid, silent, and
dignified. This was the day for the white men to make
their talk and the Seminoles waited in polite silence for
the agent to address them. The Negro Abraham, interpreter
for old Micanopy, sat with them. He possessed a remarkably
high, broad forehead, but a permanent squint in his right
eye gave a sinister look to an otherwise gentle manner.[61]

Thompson's words came slowly through Abraham to
the assembled leaders. He spoke at great length of the

58. Cohen, p. 57.

59. Boyd, *Florida Aflame*, p. 48; McReynolds, p. 141-42; Thompson to Elbert
Herring, October 28, 1834, *FTP*, XXV, 58-62.

60. McCall, p. 302; Cohen, p. 62.   61. McCall, p. 302; Cohen, p. 239.

interest that the White Father in Washington took in his children the Seminoles and of the consideration and patience that he had shown them and his pleasure at their appraisal of the new land that he had prepared for them in the West. His concern extended to the smallest detail and as his agent here in Florida, he (General Thompson) would now ask their pleasure concerning the disposition of their stock and other personals and their preference as to the mode of travel to the Territory.

The agent finished and took his seat while the interpreter slowly completed the transfer of his questions into the nearest Seminole equivalent. His listeners did not register their confusion as mention was made repeatedly of a *treaty* at Fort Gibson but the closing questions made the meaning of the agent clear. He was under the misapprehension that their marks had indicated willingness to leave their homes for the western lands. Impassively the Seminole audience rose silently to their feet and left the council-room for their own encampment. They would return on Friday for their reply.

Then once more they gathered at the office near Fort King. After suitable silence, Holata Mico, a war chief, spoke the opening lines of conciliation: "We come to make our talk today. We were all made by the same Great Father, and are all alike his children. . . . Therefore we are brothers, and as brothers, should treat together in an amicable way, and should not quarrel and let our blood rise up against each other. . . ."[62] His few words were more invocation than argument, asking that reason and friendliness prevail, though differences might arise.

Now rose Jumper, advisor to Micanopy, and a man whose voice was listened to in the highest councils of the Indians. He stood a full six feet tall, as lean and hard as a pine, and he addressed himself to Thompson, his peculiar musical voice giving expression to his small black eyes.[63]

62. Cohen, p. 57.
63. John T. Sprague, *The Origin, Progress, and Conclusion of the Florida*

At the treaty of Moultrie, it was engaged that we should rest in peace upon the land allotted to us for twenty years. All difficulties were buried, and we were assured that if we died, it should not be by the violence of the white man, but in the course of nature. . . . The deputation stipulated at the talk of Payne's Landing, to be sent on the part of the nation, was *only authorized to examine* the country to which it was proposed to remove us and *report* to the nation. We went according to agreement, and saw the land. It is no doubt good, and the fruit of the soil may smell sweet and taste good, and be healthy but it is surrounded with bad and hostile neighbors, and the fruit of bad neighborhood is blood, that spoils the land, and fire that dries up the brook. . . . When we saw the land, we said nothing: but the agents of the United States made us sign our hands to a paper, which *you say* signified our consent to remove; but *we* considered we did no more than say we liked the land, and when we returned, *the nation would decide.* We had not authority to do more. Your talk is a good one, but my people cannot say they will go. We are not willing to do so. If their tongues say yes, their hearts cry no, and call them liars.[64]

Jumper took his seat, his face as impassive as when he had begun. Not an Indian had moved. Like statues they had listened to Jumper's words and now, by prearrangement, Charley Emathla stood in turn. Here was no warrior but a farmer, intelligent and thoughtful. His farm lay only a short distance from Fort King, at Wetumpka, and his words would reflect the feelings of many men.

> . . . I was not at the treaty of Moultrie, but it was not made by *children. Great men* were the actors in it. That treaty is *sacred.* It stipulated that we should receive the annuity for twenty years, and enjoy the land defined to us. The time has not expired—*when it* does, then we can make

War (New York, D. Appleton & Co., 1848; reprinted in the Floridian Facsimile and Reprint Series, Gainesville, University of Florida Press, 1964), p. 97; Cohen, p. 239.

64. Cohen, pp. 57-58.

a *new* bargain. There may be slight causes of complaint
between the white man and the red, but they are not
enemies. . . . When a man has a country in which
he was born, and has there his house and home, *where his
children have always played about his yard,* it becomes
sacred to his heart, and it is hard to leave it. Our Father,
the President, has repeatedly said, he views and regards us
as his children—and doesn't he know that when a man is
settled, with his little stock around him, he has some assurance of support for his little ones? But break him up and
remove him, and they must be exposed to suffer! . . . [M]y
people are around me, and they feel that while they remain
here, they can be happy with each other. They are not
hungry for other lands, why should they go and hunt them?
The country [Arkansas] is very distant. It was with difficulty
we, with firm health, reached it. How then would it be with
the sickly and infirm? . . . I view you (the Agent) as a
friend, but if we differ in opinion, *I am a man,* and *have
a right to express my sentiments.* . . . I am pleased with our
first acquaintance, and hope there will be mutual satisfaction. I am done. We will meet in council tonight, and
tomorrow we will talk again. May the Great Spirit smile,
and the sun shine on us.[65]

The meeting having been called at the request of General
Thompson, courtesy required that the Seminoles remain
until he signified that the conference was over. Accordingly,
Emathla took his seat, as it was evident that the agent would
address them again. His lean, tanned face had been no mask
for his emotions while his guests were speaking and he
shifted and fidgeted in his rough upright chair. Now he was
on his feet, talking while the interpreter was still translating
Emathla's words. Enough had been said to make it clear
that these stiff-haired, broad-faced natives were flatly
refusing to leave the land under any conditions, much less
state the manner in which they would leave. Loudly and
rapidly Thompson told them that he would not accept their

65. Cohen, p. 58-59.

talk—there was no longer any question of their leaving, but only the method by which they would go. Their father the President had great concern for them, but there was an end to patience. The treaty had been signed at Payne's Landing, the Treaty of Fort Gibson had been signed, and their own marks on those papers were the judges against them. They had agreed to sell their land and move to the West—and they *must* go. His righteous anger propelled him on and he leaned across the council table toward the impassive faces, his voice rising with his anger, perhaps spurred as much by their lack of response—by their total lack of motion—as by their obstinate unwillingness to give up their country.

To his audience, the performance was an unwarranted outburst, almost obscene, for a deliberative occasion was not the place for violent passions.[66] When his words were finished, the Seminoles rose and passed from the room, their moccasins soundless on the rough floor as they crossed the porch, followed in respectful silence down the steps and across the compound toward their own camp by their wives and waiting warriors.

The next day, in silent dignity, they returned. Once again, Holata Mico, a principal war chief, opened the talk. His few words were conciliatory, but tendered a mild reproof. ". . . I am not excited. *Our* way of doing business is to proceed coolly and deliberately, and in a friendly manner. . . ."[67] A little more, and then he deferred to Micanopy.

Here stood the least typical of Indians. The hereditary chief of the Seminoles since 1814, Micanopy was short, fat, and lazy. His face gave evidence of neither pride nor character, but instead was a swollen dark sponge of carbuncles with eyes like small dull stones. In 1825 the government agent, Colonel Gad Humphreys, had technically stripped him of power by inducing the Indians to make their chief-

---

66. Cohen, p. 59; Thompson to Herring, October 28, 1834, *FTP*, XXV, 58-59; Mark F. Boyd, "Asi-Yaholo or Osceola," *FHQ*, XXXIII (January-April, 1955), 269.
67. Cohen, pp. 59-60.

tainship elective, but their elected leader John Hicks, while exercising powerful control throughout the nation, recognized the legitimacy of Micanopy's position and in this meeting he spoke as a chief. An awkward, clumsy man, Micanopy rose to his feet with an effort.[68] "The talk of *yesterday* is still the talk of *today*. . . . *When* the twenty years from the date of the treaty of Moultrie are ended, we may consent to remove. *Now* we cannot do so. If suddenly we tear our hearts from the homes round which they are twined, our heart-strings will snap. By time, we may unbind the chords of affection—we cannot pluck them off, and they not break."[69]

Simply, abruptly, he was done. Inertia had long been a habit with the old chief, and he was as much opposed to emigration as he was to war. His vacillating policies had gradually caused his power to slip to his advisers, mainly to lean, hard Jumper, ten years his junior and married to Micanopy's sister. Jumper again faced the gray-haired white chief, and he repeated his objections of the previous day. There was no help here for Thompson.

Then Charley Emathla, a subchief of the Nation, respected by both the Indians and white men as intelligent and honest, spoke:

> . . . Our Agent told us yesterday, we had not answered *his* talk, and what we gave as a reply, could not be received. [But] if we intended to go, *then* it would be proper the points be [*sic*] proposed to us should be decided upon. But why quarrel about dividing the hind quarter, when we are not going to hunt. Why strain the water, when you are not thirsty. . . .The treaty [at Payne's Landing], was one of the white people's making. I agreed to go and see the country, I went. I got on board a strange vessel, where I had never been before. It made me sick, till my heart turned in me. I endured it, because *my nation might be benefitted* by the

68. Sprague, p. 97; Cohen, pp. 64, 238; Williams, pp. 214, 272.
69. Cohen, p. 60.

result of the expedition; but how will not the women and children suffer in such a passage? . . . We were ill used by the Agent. We were abandoned when sick on the road. We were sometimes made to walk on foot. If the *few* on that expedition were exposed to such hardships and ill-usage on their journey, how much more suffering must there be, when the *whole nation* is moving in a body. . . . At Moultrie, my head men and yours agreed that all ill feeling should be buried, and a lasting peace take place between us. The tomahawk was to be under ground, and the smoke of the calumet was to rest forever above it. We agreed that if we met with a brother's blood on the road, or even found his dead body, we should not believe it was by human violence, but that he had snagged his foot, or that a tree had fallen upon him—that if blood was spilled by either, the blood of the offender should answer it. That we were always to meet as friends and brothers, without distinction of rank; and that if one was hungry, the other should share his bread with him. When a man calls another his friend, *let him be poor or mean as he may,* he ought to yield to him his rights, and not say that *he* will judge for that other, and compel him to do as *he* pleases. Yet while you say you are our *friend,* you tell us we *shall* go to the West. . . . When our Headmen visited Washington, the President . . . assured us we should not be disturbed in the enjoyment of the territory marked out to us, while we observed the stipulations of our treaty. We have done so![70]

The room fell silent. On one side the agent, his features drawn and hard, leaned on the council table flanked by his assistants, each aware that in the blank but unyielding faces before them rested the obstacle to irreversible government commitments. From the President down through his agent, emigration for the Seminoles was the word and General Thompson was the voice. He had tried reason, coercion, and anger, but these heathen insisted on putting everything on a footing of basic human understanding. There might be papers written by the white men, and under pressure

70. Cohen, pp. 60-62.

they would sign them, but when the presents had been exchanged, when drinks were drunk and hands shaken, here they sat, and they dared to say "No" because they were right. This *was* their land, and no reshuffling of papers, regardless of how rapidly or skillfully done, could make them say it wasn't. And all his papers and his presents and his words hadn't really changed them. Damn their flat, ugly faces— they must be made to understand that they *would* leave, every last one of them. Their only choice was Indian Territory or a grave. Just one problem: how did a Christian, an officer, and a gentleman explain to a bunch of Indians that there was no point in further discussion, that his government used words and paper only to cover invasion and murder? Well, that's what they were paying him for.

Thompson looked up as a final spokesman for the Seminoles rose lithely to his feet. This was a young Indian to be in council—he wasn't much over thirty and the very antithesis of old Micanopy who sat beside him. Thompson had seen him around the agency many times but he had no official position, either through heredity or election. He was a young and handsome man, reputed to have a share of white blood and certainly his complexion was lighter than his companions.[71] He was shorter than the grim-faced Jumper, standing only five feet eight inches tall, slim and muscular, his body relaxed, his eyes deep and restless. Beneath the flower-patterned cloth wrapped turban fashion around his head, Indian-black hair fell across his forehead nearly to his brow and on the sides it reached to the jawline. The face was strong and the eyes intelligent. Thompson groped a moment for his name and then he remembered. They called him Osceola.[72]

He spoke now, neither loud nor forceful. His voice was clear and a little shrill, but there was something about him that made what he had to say important. At a private session

71. Boyd, "Osceola," p. 254; Cohen, p. 235.
72. Thompson to Herring, October 28, 1834, in *FTP*, XXV, 59; Boyd, "Osceola," p. 270; Cohen, p. 62; Williams, p. 216; McReynolds, pp. 146-47.

of the chiefs, Thompson knew this young Seminole had urged united opposition to emigration. Until this morning he hadn't known that the words had had such telling effect.[73] Holata Emathla and others had indicated that they might be convinced of the advantages of the move to the West, but after Osceola's words, they were all united against it. Minutes before, as Micanopy had prepared to rise, the agent had noticed Osceola speaking to him and now the interpreter advised him that his words had been an admonition to the old chief to be firm.[74] The words addressed to Thompson in Seminole were now being translated: *"The sentiments of the nation have been expressed. . . .* The People in Council have agreed; by their Chiefs they have uttered: it is well, it is truth, and must not be broken. . . ." He looked directly at the agent. "When *I* make up my mind, I *act*. If I *speak*, what I say, I *will* do . . . *what I resolve, that I execute. . . .*"[75] As the words came through in translation, there was no doubt left in the mind of the agent that this was the voice of the Seminole Nation, and somehow the breeze of late October seemed a little cooler. The conference was over.

General Clinch, humane but determined, and as inept as he must be in dealing with people whose ways were as incomprehensible to him as the wind, ordered abandoned forts reoccupied throughout the state and reinforcement of those forts already manned. Perhaps a show of force would make it clear to the Seminoles that there was no logic to resistance and that whatever course was taken, it would end in removal to the West.

Of prime importance was the bolstering of the forces at Fort King, and Major Francis Dade was perhaps as good a man for this mission as any other—maybe better than most. He knew the route, and there probably wasn't an

73. Boyd, "Osceola," p. 269.
74. Thompson to Herring, October 28, 1834, *FTP*, XXV, 59.
75. Cohen, p. 62.

officer in the territory with his unique experience, for he had passed this way before. Ten years ago word had come down from Fort King that the Indians were showing increasing hostility. Troops were needed to reinforce the post in case of attack. Francis Dade (he was a captain then) had been chosen to make the march from Fort Brooke with one hundred men and a six-pounder. Less than a week later they had arrived safely at the agency; the threat had passed and the uneasy peace had lasted, more or less, for ten years. Perhaps now the same play would win the same game.[76]

Beneath his chivalry and dash, the major was fully aware of his responsibility and as the men settled into the semi-silence of the march he had time to reflect on his present situation and to make his plans. By nightfall they could easily reach the Little Hillsborough River where they would make their first camp. The bridge might be out but they had axes with them and plenty of men, and pine logs made a good raft. It was the other rivers—the Big Hillsborough and both branches of the Withlacoochee—that would be a problem. It was unlikely that the small roving bands of hostile Seminoles that had been plaguing the territory for the past two months would have spared the three main bridges on the military highway. The road was the backbone of military logistics and the bridges were its weakest points. Theoretically, one Seminole or a hundred of them could be right here, behind the pines or lying in ambush beneath cover of palmetto, but it was at the river crossings that they could expect attack—if it were to come. The Little Hillsborough should be safe enough—it was really little more than a creek—but the others would be a different matter. With men strung out across cold, chest-high water, part of the force on one bank and part on the other, they'd be in real danger. But they would cross those rivers—one way or another—when they came to them.

The advance guard was out, leading the way as the road wound north and east through flat, rising land, and Dade

76. McCall, pp. 147-48.

could see the customary flanking guards as they paralleled the detachment through the palmetto, a few hundred feet out on either side. The road itself was twenty feet wide and one hundred miles long, cleared of all trees, stumps, and palmettos. It was wide enough for any military equipment or command; but it was soft and, in dry seasons like this, hard marching. There was little risk that hostiles would be here in the vicinity of the fort, but there was equally little profit in taking chances. Ten years of almost continuous duty in the Territory taught a man that you couldn't second-guess a Seminole and many a trooper had lost his scalp in these same pine barrens because he hadn't learned that his enemy would attack as much by impulse as by logic. His job was to get this detachment through to the relief of Fort King with the least possible delay, and complain or not, the men would guard the flanks, put up breastworks at night, and stand guard. He would back his boast that he could march with impunity through the Indian Nation with one hundred men.[77] Fate had given him the chance once before and he had proved himself right. With stout-hearted men behind him, a little luck and enough courage, he'd make it again.

The transfer of command had delayed their departure from the fort but it was still early and they had put the first mile behind them. The air was a cool fifty-four degrees with a breeze out of the northeast right in their faces.[78] The sun was climbing now, shining through the clear sky like a brass button on a blue coat. The men were hitting a stride that they could keep up for hours and the steady tramp of boots

77. Gardiner file; Cohen, p. 231.

78. "Diary of the Weather" at Fort Brooke, East Florida, for the quarter ending the thirty-first day of December, 1835. Assistant Surgeon H. L. Heiskell, in his meticulous weather diary, gives the temperature three times for each day, at 7:00 A.M., 2:00 P.M., and 9:00 P.M., in addition to wind direction, notation as to "Fair" or "Cloudy" skies, and under "Remarks" such comments as "Showers during the day," "Rain," and so forth. As the command proceeds north from Fort Brooke, the weather conditions have been extrapolated from a study of current comparisons between Tampa and points north and this gauge then applied to Dr. Heiskell's measurements for December, 1835, and those at Fort King.

stirred the light sand of the road until it hung in the air to
settle on the bright palmetto blossoms along the way. A
jingle of harness and the dry creak of leather, the screech
of axles and the drum of footsteps—the wild things of the
wood paused to listen, for an army was passing.

By the time the 100-yard-long column reached the ridge
where the pine woods began some two miles from the fort,
the glare of direct sunlight in the crystal air began a welcome
warming. Ransom Clarke wiped his damp nose on his
sleeve while the man to his left marched in his shadow.
They passed the spring a few yards off the road where a trail
led down to the sinkhole. The people of the fort had
been coming here for their water since 1824 when Colonel
George Mercer Brooke, Captain Dade, and Lieutenant
George Archibald McCall had first established Cantonment
Brooke.[79] Sloshing in their canteens now was water from
the spring, carried to the fort in barrels on a mule-drawn
wagon and distributed the night before.[80] They would pass
plenty of water along the road but the clear substance of
the spring was preferable to the dark water of the rivers
or the stagnant stuff of ponds.

The beginning of a long day's march was not conducive
to conversation and each man marshaled his strength and
endurance for the test of travel. Long and sandy miles lay
ahead and a gradual shifting and settling of packs and rifles
was taking place all along the column. A twisted shoulder
strap, a loose belt—these must be adjusted before they could
cause trouble, for the Indians and the weather were enough
to worry about without having blisters, too. Any soldier who
had done even a two-mile training hike knew that what
seemed like a light pack on the parade ground gained weight
with every mile. These men were mostly hardened veterans
and they carried few personal possessions; the greatcoat and
bedroll in their haversacks and some two pounds of food

79. McCall, pp. 127-36; Grismer, pp. 54-60.
80. George M. Brooke to Jacob Brown, February 5, 1824, Records of the War
Department, Office of the Adjutant General, letters received; Covington, p. 326.

were burden enough. The issue was three-quarters of a pound of pork or bacon—unless they were lucky enough to get beef—and eighteen ounces of hard bread. Then there was a share for each man of the wagon-drawn supplies—two quarts of salt, four quarts of vinegar, eight quarts of peas or beans, four pounds of coffee, and eight pounds of sugar per day—to be rationed out to one hundred men.[81] Nothing fancy, but it would keep the troops going for the hundred miles ahead.

The land lying north of the bay had no more striking features of terrain than the wrinkles in a blanket. Through the straight pines that covered the land in endless ranks the men could still see the bay glinting like a coin tossed in the sun. They had cleared its northern tip by a mile and a half and the road was straight, swerving only to avoid a shallow pond thick with marsh grass or a low hill bulging perhaps ten feet above the level plain. Their course was directly northeast for the next twenty miles, roughly paralleling the Hillsborough River as it turned and twisted to the sea. They had left it when they left the fort and now it was four miles away, but they would cross the intervening arc and rest tonight where it was joined by the Little Hillsborough, five miles ahead.[82] This was low country and even during the dry winter season there were more swamps than dry land—good country for an ambush. A disciplined army was fine on a European battlefield but it could never really come to grips with an enemy who could strike from the fastness of a cypress swamp and disappear before a civilized man could return the fire.

Major Dade watched both the countryside and the men; the latter seemed confident, the former, peaceful. He knew the first fifty miles would be the worst; after that they would be in high country where troops could maneuver. But they

---

81. Jacob Rhett Motte, *Journey Into Wilderness: An Army Surgeon's Account of Life in Camp and Field During the Creek and Seminole Wars, 1836-1838*, ed. James F. Sunderman (Gainesville, University of Florida Press, 1953), pp. 13, 253.
82. Belton to Jones, January 1, 1836.

had a perfect day to start with—the sun was warming as they crossed the infrequent clearings and he could look with confidence along the bobbing black forage caps of his men. The two columns moved apart as he passed and the rich green palmetto fronds rustled as the men's boots brushed against them. High up in the pines the birds flitted and scolded, cardinals and bluebirds looking like Christmas ornaments against the short green needles, while the gray squirrels with white bellies clung to the flaky bark and looked down on the intruders with eyes like black beads.

From the rear, the whip-crack and curses of the driver drifted up the line with increasing intensity as he coaxed and goaded the ox-team to greater effort. Wheeling toward the rear, Dade trotted his mount down the line past the last of the marching troopers; the gap between the column and the oxen had been growing steadily wider. The animals were scrubby stock bought from the settlers at the fort and their strength and understanding were both exhausted. The thousand-pound burden of cannon, carriage, and limber was worse than dead weight, the natural drag made infinitely greater by soft, loose sand in which the iron-shod wheels were cutting tracks six inches and more deep. The driver walked beside the lead ox, jabbing him incessantly with a goad, but it was apparent that the team had nearly given out. Already the command was behind schedule, tied to the lagging pace of these beasts that acted as an anchor on the rear of the column. They had made only four miles though the sun was almost straight overhead. The major halted the column with a command that was repeated up the line. The officers gathered and he gave instructions: take the oxen off the gun, put them in harness to the wagon in place of the single horse, and abandon the six-pounder here for the present. When they got into camp they could send back to Captain Belton for additional horses to pick up the cannon and bring it on. And hurry it up.[83]

83. This event is based on Belton's letter (Belton to Jones, January 1, 1836), in which he states ". . . I heard from Major Dade, pressing me to forward the

The trooper driving the supply wagon brought it to the rear of the column and men immediately set to work releasing all five animals from harness and switching the oxen to the wagon. The four-foot cannon was wheeled off the road and abandoned, breech elevated and muzzle down.

Word was passed from the rear guard that two riders were approaching from the direction of the fort. Men scrambled to their feet and officers swung into their saddles. Only four miles out wasn't a likely place for Indian trouble, but one Indian seen might mean a hundred Indians in the brush. If you grew old here, it was because you didn't let down your guard—ever. From his saddle, Dade could see a flash of blue through the pines. Probably a messenger and guard—no Seminole would approach in so obvious a fashion. But then the second rider was a Negro. The uniformed rider raised his arm in signal as he swept past the rear guard and slowed as he saw the group on horseback in the road.

Squinting against the sun, Captain George Gardiner and the Negro reined in near the major, officers exchanging salutes. It seemed that a decision had been made at the fort to return the schooner *Motto* to Key West for supplies and he had arranged for Mrs. Gardiner to be on it. Dr. Benjamin Franklin Nourse, who had come up from Key West with Dade,[84] was returning with her and would

---

6 por [pounder] . . . it having been left from the failure of the team, 4 miles out." This area is still undeveloped and examination has shown it to be sandy soil with little growth. The dry winter of December, 1835, would have left the sand exceedingly soft and loose, quite incapable of providing firm support for the burden of the cannon and the oxen. As to the quality of the oxen, it seems unlikely that there would have been enough choice among the scant stock of the military or civilians at Fort Brooke to assure strong, sound, and sturdy animals—it is far more likely that they were the scrubby stock described, and poorly suited to the military service to which they were put. Yet, they did continue in harness to the wagon, so it does not appear that they were sick, or injured. Hence, the conclusion drawn by the author seems (at least to him) to be the most likely in the light of the conditions that existed and in view of the few recorded facts. However, it should be made entirely clear that this conclusion is assumed, in an effort to bridge from one fact to another—the oxen did "fail," yet when released from the cannon, continued.

84. G. Fitzpatrick to R. K. Call, January 8, 1836, *House of Representatives Document #278*, p. 31.

soon have her in the hospital. Her father and the children would be with her and he was thus enabled to join the command. As for the Negro, Louis Pacheco, Belton had sent him along as interpreter since he had some knowledge of the Seminole tongue.[84a] Handshakes and salutes were exchanged as each of the officers came up then and a momentary euphoria brushed them all. Gardiner was an able and experienced officer, ranking even Dade in years of service, and they appreciated the sense of duty that had brought him to this post of danger when he could as easily have sailed with his wife on the schooner to comfort and safety.

With his graying hair showing beneath his cap and his short figure made dumpy by his plain citizen's coat, Captain Gardiner faced the major and his blunt protestations were clearly audible to the men as they argued. Dade, with unfailing military courtesy, proffered the command to the captain, originally in charge of it. Gardiner, with characteristic bluntness, refused to supersede the major. And so it remained—the command still led by Major Francis Dade, but increased in number and morale by Captain Gardiner.[85]

Unencumbered by the cannon and accustomed to the pull of a wagon, the oxen plodded steadily on. The temperature

84a. Though Pacheco has been generally considered guide (rather than interpreter) by contemporaries and historians and subject to obloquy during his long life for having supposedly led Dade and his command into a trap, the author feels that the facts bear up the statement that he was employed (and acted) solely as interpreter. Belton states in a report to Clinch on December 23, ". . . I have just employed and sent an interpreter to the detachment." Further, it is hardly credible that Major Dade, who had traveled this road before, would have needed a guide, but if he had, there was Ransom Clarke in his own command who had been for some months the mail carrier on the Fort Brooke-Fort King run. On the other hand it is doubtful whether any man of the command had any knowledge of the Seminole language—a lack that would have been critical if peaceful confrontation had been made—while Pacheco was an intelligent and even educated man for his race and time and had served as interpreter for various commanders at Fort Brooke.

85. Potter, pp. 102-3; McCall, p. 300; Alvord, p. 40; Cohen, p. 69; Boyd, *Florida Aflame*, p. 89. The event recounted here is not in historical question, as it is given in closely synonomous terms by Potter, McCall, and Alvord, all of whom were in a position to know the facts at first hand. The *time* of Gardiner's rejoining the command, however, is based upon reasoning that contains as much logic as the author was able to muster. It is clear, from the above sources, that Gardiner overtook the command somewhere between Fort Brooke and the Little Hills-

had risen to sixty degrees when the command was given to halt for the midday meal. For a hundred yards along the road the men settled in place and from their haversacks made a meal of meat and hard bread, washed down with coffee ladled out to each man in his tin cup. Below them, at the foot of the low slope they had been traveling, sunlight sparkled on a shallow pond, a half-mile of water full of saw grass and surrounded by patches of marsh. The officers ate from their personal mess chests carried on the wagon, their ration the same as the men's though they were allotted more—two, three, four or more rations, depending on their rank.[86] They had put another mile or so behind them, leaving the low and seasonally marshy ground near the bay, and while they ate they could look out across the rising pine land that climbed from the sea. They had crossed a little ridge that rose fifty feet above the bay and they rested along its sloping side as it wound north and east toward the Little Hillsborough. A quarter of a mile east, at the foot of the hill, a spread of marsh grass indicated the bottom of a springtime lake, the edge of a vast area that stretched south along the bay, where only mosquitoes and saw grass thrived. Back along the road the gently sloping land that led to the fort was dotted with the stark leafless trees killed in the bitter winter of a year ago.[87] And sometimes, between the trees, living and dead, and across the open savannas, a soldier here and there caught a last glimpse of the open sea.

By early afternoon they reached the end of the ridge they had been following and started down the quarter-mile slope that led to the Little Hillsborough, a narrow stream that drained the swamps east of the main river. Major Dade ordered the slave Louis Pacheco to push on to the bridge

---

borough River (a distance of seven and a half miles), but the encounter at the time and place of the failure of the team, "four miles out," is an assumption by the author. Since we know there had to be a halt (of uncertain length) to switch the oxen to the wagon, it would seem that there was considerably more likelihood of his arrival during this interruption than otherwise.

86. Motte, p. 253.

87. Motte, pp. 156, 292-93; T. Frederick Davis, "Early Orange Culture in Florida and the Epochal Cold of 1835," *FHQ*, XV (April, 1937), 232-39.

and examine the surrounding area for signs of Indian activity while the column continued slowly along the road. The previous day friendly Indians of Holata Emathla's band had reconnoitered the locality at the order of Captain Belton and their report had been that the bridge was all right, but it wouldn't hurt to double-check. Captain Upton S. Fraser, commanding B Company, Third Artillery Regiment, and lately in command at Fort Brooke, protested as the Negro moved forward alone, but the major saw no reason for concern.[88] The view was relatively clear to the bridge and attack was unlikely from the scant brush, especially upon a single black man. And if he got in trouble, help was right here.

From the moment his master's widow had hired him out this morning to accompany the command the thirty-five-year-old Negro had been apprehensive. Captain John Casey had come to their place south of the fort where Andrew Pacheco had established residence and made an agreement with Mrs. Pacheco to pay twenty-five dollars a month for his services and upon their arrival at the fort Captain Belton had sent him out to overtake the command. Francis Dade

88. Louis Pacheco (or Lewis Fatio), statement in the Austin (Texas) *Commercial Journal* (August, 1861), quoted by McKay, II, 480. Pacheco states that "[Major Dade] sent me ahead to examine at the Hillsboro Bridge, about seven miles above Tampa, where I found the bridge burned, etc. . . ." In the absence of other sources on this point, the author has accepted the greater portion of Pacheco's statement with reference to his being sent forward to "examine," but has not in this case accepted his report on the condition of the bridge in the face of conflicting evidence. Pacheco's statement came twenty-six years after the events narrated, while Belton states clearly in his letter of January 1, 1836, that "three out of four bridges are destroyed [between Fort Brooke and Fort King]," which indicates that one was still standing. As we shall see, Belton was to have direct contact with five different men from the command after the stop at the Little Hillsborough River, which should have enabled him to have the facts concerning which bridges were standing and which were not. (However, Belton's statement seems to have its flaws, as we shall indicate, and it seems that the bridges had been reported as being "burnt," which Belton assumed meant "destroyed," which evidently was not entirely the case, the fire in one other instance not having completed its work.) Assuming then that at least one of the four was usable, it seems more likely that this one, over the little river, which was both closer to a white settlement (Fort Brooke) and therefore more dangerous for Seminole marauders to approach, and on the other hand smaller and less important to the whites than any of the other three, hence less important to destroy from the Indian point of view, was the one standing.

had assured him that there was no hostility on the part of the Indians—but neither of them believed it. Through a succession of masters Pacheco had gained fluency in English, French, and Spanish, both written and spoken, plus a knowledge of Seminole and he felt pretty sure that an educated slave would arouse little sympathy in the major. Perhaps it was only common sense and military caution that the major should send him ahead to look for signs of danger, but Pacheco took it as a sign that the major considered him expendable. Even Captain Fraser had remonstrated with him for it, telling him that he was putting the Negro in considerable danger; but the slave wanted no trouble with white men or red, so he kept silent and walked apart.[89]

The officers watched as he moved slowly about the approach to the bridge, frequently stooping to examine the ground, his small dark figure discernible only by its motion against the brown vegetation. Beyond him the trestles of the little bridge looked spiderlike against the river, which shone like a dark blue ribbon in the winter sun. Completing a hasty inspection, Pacheco returned to confirm that the bridge was still intact, but that there were Indian tracks thick in the vicinity and a cow had been killed and cut open near the edge of the river. Dade listened in silence, then with a gesture dismissed the slave.

In a grove of live oak trees three hundred feet from the water the advance guard halted and word was passed to fall out and make camp for the night, their bivouac area spread on the narrowing wedge of land that commanded a good view on three sides, with the open road behind them and a water barrier in front. To their left, the low land bordering the Big Hillsborough began four hundred yards away and led an equal distance to the river itself, three hundred feet across even in this dry season of the year. And on the right, the foot of the hill faded into impassable swamp nearly a

89. Giddings, pp. 101-2; Kenneth W. Porter, "Three Fighters for Freedom," *Journal of Negro History*, XXVIII (January, 1945), pp. 65-72.

mile wide, affording protection against a surprise attack
of any size. If trouble came, it must come down the road.

As soon as Gardiner and Fraser had deployed their
respective companies, axes were brought up from the supply
wagon and parties were sent back into the pine woods beside
the road on log-cutting detail. Within minutes the steady
ring of axes could be clearly heard, punctuated by cries of
warning as hundred foot pines were brought to earth. The
great trunks, some of them three feet thick, were cut into
movable lengths and rolled into camp to form the nucleus
of the fires. Others, smaller in diameter, were left full length
and used in the low barricade that rapidly took shape
around the entire bivouac area. The major and Dr. Gatlin,
with other officers not involved in the routine of setting up
camp, had already begun making their meager arrangements for the night. Mess chests were brought out
and blankets spread. Men who performed duties of orderlies
unsaddled the horses and put them on the picket line. Dade
hastily scratched out a message for Captain Belton, giving
their position and apprising him of the abandonment of the
six-pounder. He urged him to send a team of horses to bring
the cannon into camp without delay. It was still midafter-
noon and there was enough time to make it. Lieutenant
Alvord was assigned the job of carrying the message back
to the fort; he had time only to bid his fellow officers goodby
before remounting. With the addition of Captain Gardiner
the command was overstaffed and Benjamin Alvord would
remain at Fort Brooke. He was a young man, only twenty-
two, and fate had plucked him by the sleeve. With the
major's message, and well mounted, he moved through the
troops along the road and then was lost to sight—in his
saddlebags the major's note, and in his head directions from
two of the officers to settle their affairs in case they did not
get through.[90]

90. In Belton's letter on January 1, he states: ". . . From [the Little Hills-
borough] I heard from Major Dade, pressing me to forward the 6 por
[pounder]. . . ." Unfortunately, Captain Belton failed to mention the name of the

Through the late hours of the afternoon the cutting of trees continued with the steady sound of chopping. When one crew began to tire it was replaced by a detail of fresh troopers while others trimmed the fallen pines and cut them to length. The larger trees were laid side by side in the center of the camp to form the base of a pyramid of logs that gradually rose five to six feet high and extended the length of the bivouac, some seventy or eighty feet. Along the base of this pile were placed lightwood knots, the pitch-filled hearts of pine tree forks that would ignite the pile within minutes when the flame was applied. Room was left up and down each side of this vast log pile for the men to lie with their feet toward it and their heads resting on a single line of logs placed ten feet away. Still farther back and encircling the camp was a log barricade, rising now to a height of three feet, that would slow any attack and provide fair cover behind which the men could crouch to fire.[91]

By half-past four the sun had dropped from sight across the Big Hillsborough and the huge oaks in and out of the bivouac stood in black relief against the soft pink of the western sky; from the east, night was rising darkly against the hard pale blue of the upper sky and a scant quarter-moon sat upon the trees. Along the pyramid of logs a few men knelt with their muskets, the vents or touch-holes stopped up with small wooden plugs to prevent firing; a flash of powder in the pans and the chunks of lighter flut-

---

messenger who brought the communication, and the designation here of Lieutenant Benjamin Alvord as that man is an assumption based on the following: In one of the documents in the monument to "Dade and His Command" that stands on the grounds of the Military Academy at West Point, the author of the document, who recounts briefly the story of Dade's journey, states that "The writer of this accompanied the Detachment to their first encampment." Again, the author of said document does not identify himself but is believed to have been Alvord, who was definitely at the Fort at the time the command was making up, was an officer of the Fourth Infantry under Dade, and, subsequent to the disaster, spoke and wrote of it with accuracy and a feeling of intimacy for the men and events. Certainly, the instructions to settle the affairs of two officers indicate that the man returning to the fort was an officer himself, and with the available knowledge concerning the officers who could have accompanied Dade, Alvord seems a likely choice.

91. Motte, pp. 49, 74.

tered fiercely against the rusty logs.[92] The smell of fresh
pine was clean in the chill air of the dying day and men
warmed themselves along the cheerful blaze, hard, dirty
hands gripping cups of scalding coffee and shrugging back
into greatcoats that had been shed in the exertion of cutting
wood. A stark but filling dinner of field rations had been
prepared and eaten with good appetites and except for guard
duty, the day's efforts were over. Already, as the fires grew
bigger, flames stabbing at the night and black smoke rising
in a rush from burning pine sap, men were rolling into their
six-and-a-half-foot blankets,[93] to lie staring into the flames
and to exchange the comments of rough and lonely men.
Slowly fatigue and silence claimed them one by one until
only a few still stood, faces ruddy in the firelight, shoulders
hunched against a cold wind from the Little Hillsborough
River, while at their feet their fellows sought their separate
dreams.

Apart from the men, Major Dade and his officers talked
quietly over their rum or coffee. Gold watches[94] glittered
in the firelight as the time was checked with increasing
frequency. It was after eight o'clock. Alvord had been gone
nearly six hours. Assuming that he had gotten back to Fort
Brooke safely and that Captain Belton had been able to
procure horses and harness on short notice, the hoped-for
team should be along any time now with the six-pounder.
For Dade, the significance of the safe arrival of the gun
would be as much in the fact that it indicated that communication was still open as in the weapon's possible value
against the Seminoles; but then he was an infantry officer.
Gardiner, Fraser, and the rest put a lot of confidence in
cannonballs.

When the alarm was finally given by one of the six
sentinels posted one hundred yards and more outside the

92. McCall, p. 192.
93. *Army and Navy Chronicle*, III (December 8, 1836), 368.
94. Excerpt from correspondence of the *Darien Telegraph*, quoted in Charleston, S.C., the *Courier* (March 11, 1836), p. 4.

entrenchment[95] it was greeted with both apprehension and relief. It *should* be the six-pounder, but it *might* be something else. Quick orders placed men in position behind the redoubt, weapons at the ready and gritty fists knuckling sleep from tired eyes. The sound that brought the alarm came clearly from the direction of the road down which they had come and attention was centered there as the last of the sleepers, blankets trailing, moved from the fire to the barrier wall. Flames from the long fire threw fitful light on the slope nearly to the crest, while the roar of its burning drowned clear perception of the approaching sound. And then the tossing heads of horses lurched into view, moving toward the camp, and in a moment more the word was passed—Alvord had gotten through and Belton hadn't failed them—the gun was here. Three men had brought the team, and while the horses were unhitched and cared for, the riders joined other men around the fire. Fond hands wheeled the little cannon through a break in the wall and positioned it facing the road. If any hostiles were planning a surprise, they'd have one in return.

With added assurance, men returned to their blankets and the hubbub died. Again only the rush and crack of the fire disturbed the night. When Private Heck sounded tattoo, the call to quarters, only the officer of the day and the men on guard duty were awake to hear him. Major Dade and his men slept safely—at the discretion of warriors that moved silently through the night.[96]

95. Statement of Ransom Clarke in Portland *Daily Advertiser* (unknown date), quoted in "Personal Reminiscences," p. 72.

96. As on so many points, there is a minor conflict here between various sources. Williams says (p. 217) that Dade asked Belton to send on a team of horses to pick up the six-pounder and that "this was done the next day, and the piece reached the camp about nine o'clock in the evening," while Captain Belton stated (Belton to Jones, January 1, 1836) "it [the team and gun] joined the column at nine that night [of the 23rd]." As in most cases of conflict between Belton and other sources, the author has relied on Captain Belton, since he clearly was in the best position to know the facts and his official report predated all others.

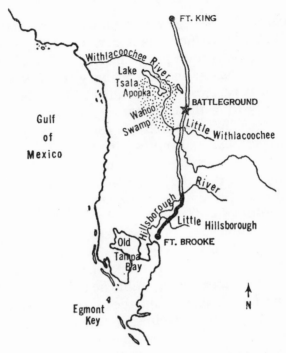

THE SECOND DAY

Thursday, December 24, 1835

DAYLIGHT was slow in coming. No light had yet broken when the bugler hammered the darkness with the strident notes of reveille, and sleeping men groggily stirred and muttered. Sergeant Cooper was on his feet before the last notes died, along with Vailing and Farley, shouting the men out of the thin comfort of their blankets to stand shivering and foot-stamping by the low-burning fire, cursing sergeants, Indians, and the cold. By the time the blue-gray of early morning was laced in the east with pink, the smell of coffee was mingling with the pine smoke, and around small fires the smell of slab bacon cut in thick, uneven slices drew men in jostling lines. As they passed the cook-fire each man got a ration of bacon to go with his handful of hard bread and strong black coffee. Breakfast was a hasty business and the first men served were quickly called out to tend the stock on the picket line near the river. Men could march and fight on empty bellies but horses and cattle would give out.

Major Dade and his officers gathered around the map while orderlies packed their mess chests, blankets, and personal effects for transport on the supply wagon. Their destination today was the crossing of the Big Hillsborough —a long trek through low and dangerous country with a good chance that they'd find the bridge over the main river destroyed when they got there. And in that case, it would be a damn cold ford through deep water.

The light was poor and bearded faces, young and old, surveyed the projected line of march through squinted eyes, trying to assess the pitfalls or advantages that lay before them. Their way led northeast by north for fifteen miles, the road relatively straight since there were few hills and only small patches of swamp to cause a detour. All day they would skirt the vast cypress swamp that bordered the Hillsborough—a morass that sprawled more than four miles wide in places. In spring and late summer the river had been known to fill the entire swamp, but now it moved calmly in the main channel. A hard day's march would bring them to the intersection of the road and river where Mr. Saunders' trading house stood by the bridge. Uninteresting country—it looked on the map like a thousand square miles of flat pine barren dotted with little lakes and swamps—fit land for wild Indians, but no country for a white man. One big lake lay about halfway down their day's route. The Seminoles called it Thlonotosassa or "Flint Abundant,"[1] and the spot where the trail passed within a few yards of it to the north would make a good spot for the midday halt.

By half-past six the firelight was fading in the pale light that filtered down through an arch of giant oak limbs. Be-

1. McCall, p. 141.

neath the trees the camp was still in deep shadow but minute by minute the sky lightened as the sun prepared to rise; it was time to move out.

The officers dispersed, Gardiner taking the map[2] and Dade moving to the front of the column. On his command the advance guard moved out toward the bridge,[3] their boots thumping loudly against the rough cypress planking as they crossed the small river. The main body waited for them to gain a lead of several hundred yards, then flankers crossed, fanned out on both sides of the far bank as the two companies in column of route moved down the embankment studded with cypress stumps and up the bridge approach. The hooves of nervous horses clattered as the company officers crossed; then came the creaking of wagon wheels and the heavy rumble of the cannon, pulled smartly along by the four horses. The little six-pounder was trundled up the bank behind the marching men, its downcast muzzle bobbing gently as it bumped along over palmetto trunks which thrust like giant brown centipedes above the sand. And last came the men of the rear guard.

At seven o'clock the thermometer at Fort Brooke stood at 60 degrees. Dr. H. L. Heiskell stepped out of his office to check the instrument, then looked up at sky as gray as the mood pervading the fort. Every hour the feeling seemed to spread that Dade and his command had taken too great a risk and it was as much in evidence in the over-loud shouts and raw humor of the men as in the anxious, withdrawn look of pretty Frances Basinger. Blame was not really attached to Captain Belton—he hadn't had any choice but to comply with the orders of the general since the complement of the fort had been reinforced by Dade and his thirty-nine, but somehow, a foreboding was gathering as thick as the fog on the bay. The order to reinforce Fort King had been suspended once before, and perhaps it should have been post-

2. Ethan Allen Hitchcock, *Fifty Years in Camp and Field* (New York and London, Knickerbocker, 1909), p. 92.
3. McCall, pp. 188-89.

poned again rather than risk the lives of the command. Not that any security was guaranteed here at the fort, though the troops remaining had been working for the past two weeks reinforcing the stockade and completing the new redoubt, named for the absent Fraser. All civilians had come within the stockade walls, rarely venturing outside, and confinement coupled with the constant dread of attack was getting on everyone's nerves. Mrs. Belton, eight months pregnant, had more reason to be upset than most, but even so, she and the other wives of the officers and men of Dade's command had declined to leave on the *Motto*.[4] Dr. Heiskell hoped they wouldn't regret it.

He returned to his ledger lying open in a circle of candlelight against the early morning gloom. He picked up his pen, dipped it in ink, wiped it carefully on the edge of the bottle, and wrote in clear, strong script: "Temperature: 60 degrees, Weather: Cloudy, Wind: N.E." He wiped the pen on a cloth and closed the book. That wind was blowing down the trail from the Little Hillsborough crossing where Dade and his men had spent the night. Too bad it couldn't bring them news. A Negro runner had left for Fort King on the fifth with the news of Captain Gardiner's arrival with his company, but it was over a month since anything had been heard from the supposedly beleaguered fort. Gardiner's brother-in-law, Colonel Alexander C. W. Fanning,[5] was in charge up at Fort King, and it was increasingly odd that they received no communication from him. He was supposedly expecting an attack at any time, hence the imperative journey of the little command, but there was no way of knowing whether he and his men were still in danger, or perhaps already dead. Certainly the silence was ominous. It would be good to believe that General Clinch was confident they would get through when he had ordered out the two companies, but as the silent hours passed the

4. Grismer, p. 78.
5. Letter from Colonel Fanning to Mrs. Fanning, December 16, 1835, Gardiner file.

mathematics of the situation kept recurring in his mind: there were at least a thousand Seminoles scattered between here and Fort King, and Dade's force numbered one hundred and eight. Courage, training, and discipline counted for a lot, but not that much. He must shake off these thoughts—for a week he would be listening to complaints and dispensing encouragement to the wives of those men on the road, and he must not show his own concern. It would be a rough week.

At Fort King, it had been a rough month for little one-armed Colonel Fanning.[6] Since November, runners coming in had given evidence that the Indians were in great numbers throughout the country for a hundred miles to the south, aware of everything that traveled the military road and capable of serious damage to anything less than a well-appointed force of perhaps a thousand men.[7] Occasional runners, and even Major John S. Lytle with a party of four mounted men, had come up from Fort Brooke without interference,[8] but Fanning knew that they had passed only on sufferance of the Indian leader Osceola. Aware that the Nation had been aroused and that a mere two companies would face serious trouble, Fanning had been desperate with anxiety to prevent their march from Tampa. Writing to his wife—Mrs. Gardiner's sister—on December 2, he said ". . . I have not put off my clothes for the last five days. Solicitude and want of sleep have much worn me down. . . ." Enlistments of his men were running out and they had no hesitancy in leaving, heading north by the Alachua Road for St. Augustine. Still other detachments had been sent to protect settlers who were in danger, leaving his force depleted. He badly needed reinforcements, but the thought of only two companies setting out to succor him was preposterous. On December 21, while Major Dade and

6. Bemrose, p. 50.
7. Belton to R. Jones, January 1, 1836.
8. *FTP*, XXV, 200; Gardiner file.

thirty-nine of his infantrymen from B Company, Fourth Regiment, were docking at Fort Brooke, Fanning had sat in his quarters one hundred miles away and written to his wife: "... I think those two companies will not leave Tampa ... that they will await the arrival of the other two companies ... or what is still more probable, all of them remain at Tampa."[9] But this was really hope, not expectation.

His fears were based on facts. It was neither luck nor accident that Major Lytle and the succeeding Negro runners had been able to get through the gauntlet of Indians. Early in December Fanning had received word that the intent of the Indians was to prevent any possible reinforcement from coming to his assistance, leaving him bottled up in the fort with less than one hundred and fifty men. They were sturdily entrenched, and Indians rarely attacked fortified positions, but any force marching cross-country would be in mortal danger. Somehow word must be gotten to the commanding officer at Tampa Bay to withhold his troops. He and his men would take their chances alone and hope for help to come from the north. In desperation, he had offered five hundred dollars to any man who would attempt to get through alone with a verbal message, but there were no takers. In an extraordinary move he had finally sent a message during the last week of November with the interpreter Indian Bill—not to Fort Brooke, but to Osceola. He explained that the paymaster Major Lytle would soon be leaving Fort Brooke to join him at Fort King, but that his payroll would have been disbursed and he would present no prize to the Seminoles nor any help to Fanning, and requested Osceola to allow Indian Bill to continue on to Tampa in order to direct the major to remain there and avoid unnecessary killing.

Osceola, skillful at human chess, was not about to throw away the advantage that was so neatly arranged. If he chose, he could send his warriors to either fort in its present con-

9. Gardiner file.

dition with a good chance of overwhelming it, and he had absolute control over travel between them. Why should he allow the northern outpost to convey their knowledge of his position to the port of embarkation where additional troops could, in an emergency, be brought in? No, the game was set up to his liking and he was in no hurry to end it; he could afford to wait. He sent the interpreter back to Fort King. "Tell Colonel Fanning that Major Lytle shall not be molested—but that no one shall live to pass *from* Fort King to Tampa."[10]

The paymaster had traveled peacefully through cold and sunny pine barrens for one hundred uneventful miles, wondering at the concern back at Brooke and arriving at Fanning's headquarters late on the afternoon of December 1, to be welcomed by the colonel who looked surprisingly tired and anxious. Fanning immediately drew the major aside and questioned him as to the state of things at Tampa Bay. Was Captain Fraser aware of the condition of the Nation—that Osceola held a tight grip on the country and that Fraser must not attempt to send troops? Lytle's protestations of a peaceful trip were brushed aside with a few chilling facts that made it clear to the startled major that he had traveled a narrow path indeed. Yes, Fraser did plan to send two companies out—his own and Gardiner's—they should be on their way by the sixteenth.

Colonel Fanning knew a moment of absolute despair. There was hardly an officer at Tampa Bay whom he didn't know personally, and it sounded from Lytle's remarks as if George Gardiner, by a cruel move of fate, would be the ranking officer who would lead them into the trap prepared by Osceola. They were all lost—unless—and this was the thought that he'd have to hold onto—unless Fraser and the others comprehended from the movements of the Seminoles in their own neighborhood the dangerous state of the whole region and suspended the orders to march.

10. *Ibid.*

Ninety miles south of Fort King the little command tramped on. All morning the skies had continued cloudy and the air was damp from impending showers while the temperature had climbed to nearly seventy. More and more greatcoats had been shed, rolled, and stuffed in the long packs that bobbed on a hundred backs. Here was no chest-out, shoulders-back, parade ground drill, but two companies of experienced troopers, shoulders hunched forward to carry the weight of body and pack evenly, legs stretching to put 30 inches behind each step; 10 miles marched and 90 to go.

The only novelty of the trip for Ransom Clarke was in traveling on foot instead of by mule or horseback as he'd done while carrying the mail, but there was a certain comfort in the familiarity of the road. For one thing, he figured the big lake up the road would be the midday stop and he could pace his energy a little better than most of the men knowing he had only a few miles to go before a halt. And he could appreciate the comparative ease and even beauty of this rolling, wooded land of morning, and dread equally the flat, featureless miles ahead of them with the afternoon. Ever since the Little Hillsborough River they had been passing through alternate stands of oak and pine that covered the low ridges which criss-crossed the countryside. Sometimes the sunlight slipped through a broken cloud to bring brilliance to the green far up in tall pines and to touch the fallen needles that lay matted beneath them with flashes of copper, filling the nostrils with the rich, pungent smell of the forest. And he was grateful too, for the ground cover of both needles and leaves, for this country seemed to be made entirely of sand and anything that would keep a man's feet from sinking in was all to the good. For a while, after the short march of yesterday, the muscles in his legs had tightened up like strips of leather drying in the sun, but gradually the soreness had faded and elasticity returned and now he was walking easily. He knew he'd feel all right as long as he kept moving, but tomorrow morning he'd do well to walk at all.

Nearby De Courcy, Thomas, Jewell, and others of his regiment strode on, seemingly impervious to afflictions of the legs. Glancing to the left at the men of the other column was reassuring. In a tight situation these were the kind of men to have with you. It was hard this morning to conjure up Indians out there behind the trees or in the grass, guns ready and dark skins daubed with paint, perhaps even now drawing a bead on him, but then death never seemed natural. He'd seen plenty of it and always it was discordant, shocking, and unnatural—whether it came as slow as a long march through soft sand, or as suddenly as a bullet. It had been that way in Mobile Bay on the night his ship went down with Lieutenant Chandler and all the ship's company, and in his memory he could still hear the awful choking cries of men in heavy winter clothing who could not swim as they threshed in icy water and called for help that didn't come. Clinging desperately to a piece of wreckage, he had watched helplessly as panic-stricken men wasted their last breath in screams while their clothing, buckled securely, overcame their wasted strength and drew them below the surface, carrying them inexorably, one by one, to the deep and muddy bottom. Then he was alone, holding on through the freezing night. It seemed like a lifetime later that he'd been sighted by the steamboat *Watchman* and hauled aboard —the sole survivor.[11] And he hadn't pulled through that one to lie down and die out here in the woods. It might not look like dangerous country, but he'd keep his eyes open every step of the way.

By ten o'clock the column was passing along the north edge of a little pond which marked the east boundary of the Fort Brooke military reservation. Now there would not even be the sustaining factor of being on a declared and mapped military reserve.[12] From here on it was Seminole country,

11. Potter, p. 107.
12. Original government survey maps and field notes, specifically those relating to township 28S, range 21E, secured from the Florida Department of Agriculture, Field Note Division, Elliot Building, Tallahassee.

plain and simple, with at least one Indian village for every white settler.

When the sun glowed dully through silver clouds directly overhead, they had traveled seven and a half miles from the little river with an equal distance still to go before making camp for the night. The general level of the land had risen slightly during the morning miles and as the long column crossed over a small knoll, Lake Thlonotosassa could be clearly seen ahead and to the right. The men on the right flank guard, little more than a hundred yards away, were passing the north shore along the edge of the great oblong of water that shone deep purple in the midday light. A breeze ruffled the surface, streaking it with silver lines while black and blue and white birds teetering on stilt-like legs stalked the shore. As they moved on they came in full sight of the lake and could look down the two mile length. Here was the source of much of the flint used by the Seminoles and probably the Timucuas before them, for the shore in many places was studded with outcroppings of the mineral. Nature's delight in sunshine and water was in great evidence here, where trees of a dozen descriptions grew to the water's edge. Magnificent cypress, towering more than one hundred and twenty feet; symmetrical magnolia whose dark green foliage rose cone-like to a height only slightly less; and scattered around among the giant trunks like stunted shrubbery were the blasted remains of frozen native orange trees with here and there a few green leaves and an occasional withered fruit.

It had been a good morning's hike, and when the halt was made, tired men dropped their packs and got out the simple rations that would keep them moving until nightfall. Coffee was brought up from the supply wagon and set to boil, the pungent smell of it whetting already keen appetites, and under the watchful eyes of the men standing guard, officers and men alike made short work of bread and meat. With few exceptions these men were veterans of at least a year's service in the field, and they wasted no time before stretching out for whatever rest was to be had before taking up the march again. There might be hostiles nearby and there might be danger ahead, but a seasoned trooper took his rest when he could get it.

The hills had disappeared. An hour past the lake they had given way to unending pine barrens that stretched flat and monotonous to the horizon, partitioned here and there with clumps of shaggy cypress standing guard over shallow ponds of sour mud. Mile after mile of tussock grass grew in ankle twisting clumps, alternating with patches of scrubby palmetto, thin and stunted from too much water. Here and there the soft, resilient sand gave way to tundra-like patches of black soil too damp for pine or oak, where the ankle-high boots of the men sank to the uppers, and tired legs grew even more weary with the pull of freeing them. To avoid these marshy spots the advance led the way in a serpentine course, trying to stay on the sand, but the farther distance of the repeated turnouts lost as much time as struggling with the muck. Many of the command, like Clarke, had at least a general idea of the course of the road, but those who had never traveled it wondered if there were any end. The sun slid down the sky directly to their left, but there was no change in the horizon where distant cypress still thrust tops like spear-points at the sky. They were beginning the approach to the Big Hillsborough, but it was still several miles ahead and only in the last thousand feet would there be any appreciable slope in the land.

Ransom Clarke crossed a little creek with an awkward jump, his feet splattering mud that had been churned into paste by the men and horses that preceded him. He remembered the creek and knew they had only another mile or two to go. And he remembered something else. Not far ahead was the pond where the body of Private Kinsley H. Dalton of the Third Regiment had been found four months before. Dalton had been on detached service as mail carrier between Forts King and Brooke and had been waylaid by a party of six Indians. The soldier's fate had a personal meaning for Clarke. He had been Dalton's replacement.

The courier had left Fort Brooke that morning of August 11 mounted on a mule and, traveling alone, was making good time toward Fort King. He, too, had crossed this little creek and Clarke knew that Dalton must have had the same thought of stopping for the night at the big river—but he never made it. Just about here he had met the small band of Mikasukis. The thought of the encounter made Clarke look sharply out through the silver-gray trunks of the cypress, just as Dalton must have done. To run or to fight must have appeared equally useless to the lone rider, and it was understood that he had approached the six with peaceful signs. They had sat still and silent while he came on, but when he reached them, just here by the pond, one of the hostiles had seized the bridle of his mule, and another had shot him from the saddle. Not content, they scalped him and then disemboweled the body. Right there was where the troopers had found his remains, a pale blur in the murky water. And he was buried close by—the grave unmarked and intentionally obscured to protect it from wolves,[13] perhaps right in the trail where the signs of burial would be quickly obliterated by the feet of passing men. It had been an act of petulance, but a man was dead, and the man was white.

Since the October meetings of last year between General Thompson and the Seminole leaders, trouble had come to be expected. Clashes between white men and red had become more and more frequent, interspersed with meetings at the agent's office at Fort King in which each side tried desperately to prevail upon the other. Slight indica-

13. Bemrose, pp. 29-30; Cohen, p. 66. Here again a study of the township plat and field notes together with examination of the land indicated the likely location where the incident occurred. The reference to wolves is based on Albert H. Roberts, "The Dade Massacre," *FHQ*, V (January, 1927), 131. For Clinch's official report of the murder see Clinch to Jones, September 12, 1835, *American State Papers* (Washington, 1861), VI, 80.

tions among a minority of the chiefs that they were considering the inevitability of removal encouraged Thompson's already strenuous effort to impress upon them that only the consideration of the white man's government kept him from unleasing overwhelming power that would harry the Seminoles until none remained; while on the other hand, the same signs of weakening drove Osceola unrelentingly to exhort his people to stay—to give not an inch of their birthright to the white man. And as he talked and traveled, his power grew.

Receipt of the agent's report of the October meetings a year ago had prompted the Secretary of War in Washington to send down an order reconvening the chiefs in December, 1834, for a repetition of the ultimatum: leave willingly, or be removed to the west by force.[14] Again, Agent Thompson had been met with flat refusal from the assembled chiefs led by Osceola and again the meeting had ended in an angry exchange between the agent and the young leader of the Indians. The conferences were taking on an increasing note of personal challenge between the gray-haired general and the Seminole whose possible white blood seemed more evident in the sweep of expression across his features when excited, coupled with the raised fist beating the air in anger, than in the color of his skin.

The frustrating meetings had continued through the winter and into the spring of 1835, though the die had been cast on the last day of the year, when the office of Agent to the Florida Indians was abolished and General Wiley Thompson became instead the Superintendent of Emigration.[15] A mood of some desperation was building among the whites. From President Andrew Jackson on down, those involved in the "due processes" with the Seminoles realized that after years of cajoling, promising, and finally threatening, the savages of the pine barrens still thought they could

14. Boyd, "Osceola," p. 271.
15. Elbert Herring to Wiley Thompson, July 10, 1834, *FTP*, XXV, 33-34; Lewis Cass to Duncan Clinch, September 11, 1835, *FTP*, XXV, 172-73.

stay on land demanded by the advance of civilization. It was absurd, and it was beginning to make a strong and impatient nation look foolish.

At last the President himself had taken a hand. In March, 1835, an assembly was called (in the absence of Thompson) by General Duncan Lamont Clinch, the military commander of all troops within the territory, to present a "talk" from the President. A gathering of chiefs heard the ultimatum.

> My children—I am sorry to have heard that you have been listening to bad council. . . . Open your ears and attend now to what I am going to say to you. They are words of a friend, and the words of truth.
>
> . . . I have never deceived, nor will I ever deceive any of the red people. I tell you that you must go, and that you will go. Even if you had the right to stay, how could you live where you are now? You have sold all your country. *You have not a piece as large as a blanket to sit down upon.*[16]
>
> Now is it not better peaceably to remove to a fine, fertile country, occupied by your own kindred, and where you can raise all the necessaries of life, and where game is yet abundant? The annuities payable to you and the other stipulations made in your favor, will make your situation comfortable, and will enable you to increase and improve.
>
> But lest some of your rash young men should forcibly oppose your arrangements for removal, I have ordered a large military force to be sent among you. I have directed the commanding officer, and likewise the agent, your friend General Thompson, that every reasonable indulgence be held out to you. But I have also directed that one-third of your people be removed during the present season. . . .[17]

To the dullest of the listening chiefs, the words of Andrew Jackson were clear—there could be no further hope of

16. Author's italics.
17. Andrew Jackson, "To the Chiefs and Warriors of the Seminole Indians in Florida" (February 16, 1835), *American State Papers*, VI, 524.

amelioration or reason. The land that had belonged to the
Seminoles by right of birth was no longer theirs. Through
ignorance and misunderstanding they had let themselves
be led to the brink of disaster by these blue-coated men
who would snuff them out as they would Okeepa,[18] the
mosquito, while they smiled and talked always of brotherhood. No, these were not friends, and the brotherhood they
offered was slow death in a far country. From this brink
there was no turning back, only to one side or the other—
resistance or submission—and for resistance they must gain
time. The meager crops must be gathered for a season of
fighting—guns and powder must be collected. Without passion Jumper rose to face General Clinch and said simply that
they must have another month in order to reconvene with
a full council since many chiefs were still absent. General
Clinch, the seasoned diplomat, offered the President's "reasonable indulgence" to a simple people, and granted the
extension.

And so the embattled red men had gained another thirty
days, to reassemble on April 22. Wiley Thompson had
returned and shared the platform with Clinch, Colonel
Fanning, and three officers of the Third Artillery. The
Seminoles were represented by nearly every chief of the
tribes, led by Alligator, Jumper, Micanopy, and Osceola.
Six hundred United States troops were quartered between
the agency and the walls of the fort and several hundred
Indians had accompanied the chiefs.[19] With new awareness
each man listened to a rereading of the entire text of the
Treaty of Payne's Landing and then a repetition of the open
letter to the Seminoles from the President. Silence. Then
Jumper, utterly opposed to removal, spoke calmly and
quietly, reiterating the consensus among the Indians, though
he offered a disinclination toward hostile resistance if the

18. This and other Seminole words are taken from the glossary in Williams,
pp. 276-77.
19. Boyd, *Florida Aflame*, p. 51, and "Osceola," p. 272; Patrick, pp. 76-77;
Bemrose, pp. 17-24.

United States employed force to carry out its scheme for removal. Like a lost hope, the theme was repeated: we will not leave our land, but we do not want war.

Thompson was spokesman for the government. The naïve simplicity of refusal from a vastly outnumbered and backward people to the politely worded orders of a strong and determined nation was as irritating as it was absurd. Through a thin veneer of civility, the general upbraided them like children for what he termed their infidelity to agreements made at Payne's Landing and at Fort Gibson. In the frustration of the moment it was easy to push back the thought that the signatory marks of illiterate men had not always been procured with defensible methods, but Thompson's motivation now was that of most men: having gained a small position of personal security which could provide him with the amenities, and able to retain that position only if he carried out his orders within a certain framework. A clear-cut and immediate wrong he would not have hesitated to abjure above job and personal position, but he was here merely as agent for a government that would, if he failed, immediately replace him with another who might have less consideration—less sympathy, for the Seminoles. There could be no gain in listening to the still, small voice that might have placed him, in sympathy, on the other side of the plank conference table; that might have carried his voice a thousand miles from Fort King to the lonely old man who sat in his study on the second floor of the White House juggling schemes for "resettling" while he paid lip service to the Christian ethic with the words, "no one can doubt the moral duty of the Government of the United States to protect . . . preserve and perpetuate the scattered remnants of this race. . . ."[20]

The dilemma of General Thompson was the dilemma of all men: whether to raise a single, subordinate voice against the injustice of a system and thereby risk oblivion in the

---

20. James D. Richardson, *A Compilation of the Messages and Papers of the Presidents* (Bureau of National Literature and Art, 1904), III, 171.

feeble cause of justice, or by simple silence to deny the responsibility of each man to justice for all men. Wiley Thompson was no better and no worse than other men. The President had ordered that these savages must move and that was an end of it, and now righteous anger could pound the table and raise its voice.

Osceola, Jumper, and the others replied to this criticism, their voices rising unnaturally with fervor. Then Thompson was on his feet again, shouting them down until General Clinch brought the meeting to order and forcibly reminded the excited Seminoles that he had been sent by the President to enforce the treaty and that discussion of this point was finished—he had the troops to compel obedience and he was prepared to use them if the Seminoles remained obdurate. To forestall further argument the meeting was adjourned until the following day.

When the council reconvened on Thursday morning, April 23, old and bilious Micanopy was conspicuous by his absence. Thompson asked Jumper, as spokesman for the Indians, whether Micanopy planned to abide by the Treaty —whether he would go peaceably to the west. Micanopy, though old and at times ineffectual, was still hereditary leader of the Seminoles, and as he led, many would follow. With hesitancy, Jumper acknowledged that the old chief would not accept, as the white men interpreted them, the terms of the treaty which had been signed at Payne's Landing. Then Wiley Thompson, in his zeal for compliance, did a shocking and foolish thing.

To a hushed audience, he peremptorily declared that the names of the five chiefs who were the principal spokesmen for opposition to removal were to be stricken from the roll of chiefs. The names of Micanopy, Jumper, and Alligator were included. There was of course no taint of justice here, for no agent of the United States government had the authority or privilege of interfering with tribal law.[21] In

21. C. W. Harris to Clinch and Thompson, May 20, 1835, in McReynolds, p. 145; Sprague, pp. 84-85.

silence and in dignity, Jumper left the room. Even for precious time, there were limits to which a man could go. When he met the bluecoats again he would give them a proper reply.

And for the remaining chiefs the time for decision had also come. They could abandon all hope of remaining in this land, hoping to preserve for their wives and children some peace, some dignity in the western country—or they could attempt to march out of this council in a body and probably never make it across the compound—but they had learned a little of the white man's way and with only a modicum of talk, they affixed their names, sixteen in all, to a new paper of utter capitulation.

"We . . . voluntarily acknowledge the validity of the treaty . . . concluded at Payne's Landing . . . and the treaty concluded at Fort Gibson . . . and we . . . fully assent to the above recited treaties in all their provisions and stipulations."[22] The rules to the white man's game were difficult and costly, but slowly they *could* be learned. For just a mark on his paper they were free to return to their homes and were not expected to be ready for departure until the new year, 1836. That bought them time to gather the materials of war, the hatchets, the rifles, and the powder; to bring in the cattle and crops to store against a long winter of war; and in the evenings by a campfire, Saphka the knife could be brought to a fine edge. Perhaps they could introduce a few rules of their own into the white man's game.

Since the council of April had ended happily for the agent and for his government, the Indians, singly and in small groups, were greeted cheerfully and cooperatively by Thompson in the weeks to come. They were frequent visitors around the fort where the agent and other officers were increasingly busy with arrangements for removal. Wiley Thompson, "Superintendent to remove Seminole Indians" as he signed the April capitulation, planned to assemble the tribes at both Fort King and Tampa Bay—

22. Cohen, pp. 55-56.

those collected at the former to be transported by wagon to Fort Brooke where a general camp for the deportees would be established. Pens would be provided for their cattle until their forced sale to the government, and the fort would also serve as a depot for provisions to carry them through the three-month trip to Indian Territory. A fleet of large schooners must be gathered in Tampa Bay to transport the entire tribe to New Orleans and river steamers must be reserved for travel up the Mississippi and the Arkansas Rivers where wagons would carry them west to their new home. Food supplies must be arranged: salt pork, beef, corn, and a little wheat flour "for a change and for the sick."[23]

Amid all the bustle and letter-writing the simple and cooperative Seminoles circulated around the fort, visiting the old agency office and making a few purchases, trading fresh game and hides for cloth, a few tools, and always, more guns and powder. Even Osceola, now rated as a sub-chief, or Tustenuggee, by the Indians, was frequently in the neighborhood, often visiting Thompson in his office.

Then in May, an ugly and fateful incident occurred. Osceola had come to the fort to trade and talk. As usual, he visited General Thompson who greeted him cordially in his log office where they conversed for some time, the agent behind his desk studying the lithe young man who paced the rough plank floor. The subject turned inevitably to removal. Once again, the powerful fist of the nearly naked chief struck and slashed the air as he recalled with bitter and insulting words the broken promises of Thompson and his government. His words were abusive and insolent and they stung the more for their truthfulness. Abruptly, the tirade at an end, he turned and stalked from the office, leaving the supervisor of emigration flushed with anger. This was not the first time the Seminole had spoken with such insolence, but Thompson had warned him before that the next time would be the last.

23. Thompson to Gibson, June 3, 1835, in McReynolds, p. 148.

Immediately he ordered Colonel Fanning to place the Indian under arrest. The four soldiers assigned to the task seized him within two hundred yards of the Fort. Osceola put up a frantic resistance, shouting bitter and trenchant threats at the focus of his outrage and hate, General Wiley Thompson.[24] Finally secured, he was half-carried, half-dragged across the compound toward the fort and those who knew the Creek tongue understood his shout: "The sun is high—I will remember the hour. The Agent has had his day—I shall have mine."[25]

In the guardhouse within the fort, still fighting and clawing like a wild thing, he was placed in irons. For hours the fort echoed with the sound of his voice, screaming like a madman from the solitude of his cell.

Sometime during the long night that followed, the voice ceased. Reason struggled with rage behind the contorted features of the Seminole chief chained in the darkness. Born to virtually unrestricted freedom, he had come with ever-increasing speed within the purview of restrictions imposed by another people, resisting always, until he now found himself in a cage that was better suited for animals—the ultimate insult and shame. But for all his wild ways and lack of discipline he was a man, and almost too late he began again to reason as a man. Even Jumper, Alligator—all the others had arranged things better than this—they were at least free. Through the night Osceola nursed his hate and made his plans. Like Jumper, he would adopt what he must of the white man's way in order to effect first his freedom—then revenge. After that, if there was time, he could dedicate himself to the destruction of any and all white men, or, for that matter, any Indian who still thought that white men should be tolerated.

Slowly the overheated passions cooled and by morning Osceola was once more composed and amenable. He sent word to Thompson that he was sorry for his remarks on

24. Cohen, p. 56; Potter, p. 86; Williams, p. 216.
25. Peithmann, p. 27.

the previous day—that he begged his pardon and would like to show his good faith by being allowed to append his signature to the agreement of April 23, if he might ask, in return, his freedom. Thompson replied that he would not be released unless satisfactory security could be provided that he meant to keep the peace. Osceola sent a messenger to several chiefs who were known to be leaning toward emigration and asked that they intercede in his behalf. One of these was Charley Emathla. Sympathetic to their plea, Thompson agreed to release Osceola on his promise to return voluntarily within five days and sign the capitulation. The epitome of conciliation and reasonableness, the imprisoned chief protested his willingness to abide by the treaty and promised to bring in others of his tribe when he returned. Still doubtful, but eager to make amends, particularly where it would facilitate government policy, Wiley Thompson had the irons struck from bronzed limbs. With hope, but not much confidence, he watched the unfettered Indian leave the fort to return to his people.[26]

Wednesday, June 3, was a day of anxious waiting. Five days had passed and Osceola was due. When the cowbell in the cupola on the two-story barracks began to ring an alarm,[27] most of the residents, military and civilian, gathered near the main gate. A group of Seminoles entered the fort—seventy-nine men, women, and children—led by Osceola. Of course there were no facilities at the fort to house these people nor would there be any point in sending them to Fort Brooke when the transports would not be available until the end of the year. Nevertheless this was a satisfying expression of their willingness to go and General Thompson greeted Osceola and his people cordially. While the newcomers wandered freely about the fort Thompson returned to his office and wrote confidently, "I now have no doubt

26. Sprague, pp. 86-87; Bemrose, p. 25; Cohen, p. 65; Williams, p. 216; Boyd, "Osceola," p. 275; Thompson to General George Gibson, June 3, 1835, *American State Papers*, VI, 76.
27. "Macomb's Mission to the Seminoles," ed. Frank F. White, Jr., *FHQ*, XXXV (October, 1956), 161.

of his [Osceola's] sincerity, and as little [doubt] that the greatest difficulty is surmounted."[28]

During the summer Osceola continued to visit and on one occasion, after a friendly talk, the general presented the young subchief with the gift of a costly and handsome rifle purchased and sent by special order from Savannah.[29] Thompson was convinced that Osceola had been converted to a sensible course and hoped that the gift would help to secure a lasting reconciliation. Osceola accepted the rifle with unfeigned satisfaction. But sales of guns and powder to the Seminoles soon ceased altogether. Thompson had noticed the steady drain on supplies and estimated that the Indians had amassed an unusual store of perhaps forty or fifty kegs of powder. With this the Seminole's visits to the vicinity of the fort dwindled and throughout the Territory the frequency of violent encounters between Indians and settlers began to increase.

During June eight warriors evaded the troops who patrolled the boundary of the reservation and set out in search of game. Their luck was poor and they separated, agreeing to meet later. The larger party found and butchered a cow belonging to a settler, dressed it out and moved on, carrying the meat with them. But on the nineteenth they met, instead of their companions, a party of Alachua settlers, members of the Spring Cove Guards who had discovered the slain animal and tracked the Indians. Not realizing the seriousness of their offense to these angry, bearded white men, they allowed themselves to be disarmed at a place called Hickory Sink near Kanapaha Pond (near present day Gainesville) and under the guns of the whites they were flogged with cattle whips. Suddenly shots rang out and three of the settlers were staggered by the fire of the smaller Indian party that had arrived at the rendezvous unobserved. In the confusion that followed, one Indian was

28. Thompson to Gibson, June 3, 1835, *American State Papers*, VI, 76.
29. Boyd, "Osceola," p. 275; Newbern, N.C., *Spectator* (February 26, 1836), in *Army and Navy Chronicle*, II (1836), 199.

killed and one wounded before they retreated, taking their dead and wounded with them.[30]

The news of the encounter quickly reached General Thompson who demanded of the chiefs the delivery of the Indians involved. He was more upset than the circumstances should ordinarily have warranted for, after all, only an Indian had been killed—the white men had recovered; but the general was growing more and more concerned with each incident that arose. He had the feeling that time had been working against him since the signing of the last agreement. Under the stress of the moment most of the chiefs had signed, but there were six months ahead before the exodus. Thompson knew that some small groups among the Seminoles still did not feel bound by *any* treaty, and their stubbornness might spread through the Nation if the implied threat of the military presence was not well in evidence.

The Seminoles, too, were edgy. Led by Osceola, now accorded the status of a principal chief, they wanted nothing to upset the plan that had gained them nearly a year's respite. They would soon be well provisioned and a reckoning would come for the indignities of the years, but not yet. Promptly, the surviving Indians were surrendered at the fort. Thompson was relieved at this show of good faith and offered his prisoners to the civil authorities. Days passed and they neither claimed them nor provided subsistence for them. Somehow it began to seem a little foolish to hold unresisting prisoners whom no one wanted when they were hardly more to blame for the encounter than their white protagonists. The chiefs obviously meant well—why not let them have the prisoners back on their promise to punish them for straying off the reservation? So the warriors left the fort, and precipitant action was allayed.

But one life was still forfeit. Male relatives of the Indian who died after the action at Hickory Sink would avenge him when the time came—and it came on the eleventh day

30. Boyd, *Florida Aflame*, p. 55; Patrick, pp. 85-86.

of August when they killed Private Kinsley Dalton on the Fort King Road.

Quickly and ostentatiously the Indian leaders requested a meeting with the officers in garrison at Fort King. Only eight days after the murder twenty-seven chiefs had gathered there, their official purpose being to present a formal request that they have an agent in the west attached solely to the Seminole people and that the agent be their friend General Thompson. Holata Emathla, brother of Charley, was the sole speaker and it may have been wondered at that for one comparatively minor request, ten principal and seventeen subchiefs would appear in person, but the plea for his presence was flattering to the general and eased again the swell of fear. By the end of September General Clinch had received a flat refusal of the request from the Secretary of War[31] but by then it hardly mattered, for another month had been gained. And it would be a long time before there were any Seminoles in the West needing an agent.

On Christmas Eve, eighty miles south of Fort King, Major Dade and his command were gathered on the south bank of the Big Hillsborough River. Cautious sentries posted along the high bank watched for signs of Indians while camp was made along the trail. By the side of the road near the bluff slumped the ash-covered foundations of William Saunders' trading house, just a few stove-in barrels and broken bottles left of the supplies, the rest looted by marauding Seminoles weeks before.[32] A butchered cow lay nearby, the remains still fresh.[33] The eleven-year-old bridge presented a discouraging silhouette through the gloom of early evening, only the charred ends of hand-hewn beams pointing like great dirty fingers from the first trestle back toward the bank, small fires still guttering up and down their length.[34]

31. Cass to Clinch, September 11, 1835, *FTP*, XXV, 172-73.
32. Thompson to Herring, January 10, 1835, *FTP*, XXV, 89; Belton to Jones, December 13, 1835, *FTP*, XXV, 211.
33. McKay, II, 480.
34. Belton to Jones, January 1, 1836; Second Lieutenant James Duncan,

The Seminoles had done an adequate job, their fire consuming the approaches beyond anything that would be reparable in either materials or time and leaving only the three main trestles standing some twelve feet above the water with sections of planking still attached. To the tired eyes of officers and men alike, the ruined structure meant just one thing—they'd ford the river tomorrow. The temperature had dropped into the sixties during the afternoon—not uncomfortable on land in dry clothes, but early morning in five feet of river water would be something else.

Already crews of men with double-bitted axes were in the woods steadily cutting and the crash of timber sounded through the coming dusk. As if to push back the night, men rolled the logs together high on the bluff and soon great spires of flame lit the entire bivouac area. Once more long pines began to form an encircling barricade and the welcome smell of coffee brought comfort to tired and worried men. Troopers warmed themselves along the fire, letting the cozy heat steam the dampness from coats that had become heavy with the showers of the afternoon while food was prepared and the first shift of guard detail was called by the officer of the day.

Major Dade had determined to send another messenger to Belton at Fort Brooke to notify him of the burned bridge and to urge haste, both in sending on extra rations and ammunition, and in the departure of Major Mountfort and his company in order to effect a juncture with the command.[35] Crossing the river would take half a day at the least and he would feel a lot more secure if Mountfort could join them here and increase their number by one-half.

Quickly, the word spread that a volunteer was needed to carry the major's message back to Tampa. In the fire glow,

---

personal diary, entry for March 16, 1836, United States Military Academy Library. (Duncan accompanied the army of General Gaines who followed Dade's course some eight weeks after Dade passed.) The bridge's still being aflame is brought out by Ransom Clarke's statement in the Portland *Daily Advertiser* (date unknown) quoted in "Personal Reminiscences," p. 71.

35. Belton to Jones, January 1, 1836.

Dade looked up into the gray eyes of a young soldier standing before him. His short figure, not over five and a half feet, combined with his light complexion and tousled brown hair made him look even younger than his twenty-four years. It was a long way from the farm in Windham, Vermont, to a campfire in Florida, and Private Aaron Jewell, Company C, Second Artillery Regiment, wasn't too happy with the transition. Up in Rochester, New York, in October of last year, enlistment had seemed like a good idea with Captain Crueger's promises of winning glory, but it hadn't worked out quite that way, especially the part about the glory. There didn't seem to be much glory available in the places he'd been. And as to the girls' being taken in by a uniform —the few females clustered in their lean-tos outside Brooke in the little civilian encampment they liked to call Tampa were more interested in a soldier's pay than romance. Probably the major here and certainly the company commander Captain Gardiner knew about his desertion in January, even if it was just four days, and with two years still to go on his enlistment it ought to help out if he volunteered to carry the message back to Captain Belton.[36]

The last he saw of the command as he rode out was the cheerful tent of firelight under vast oaks and his comrades in silhouette like so many shadows in the night. His tired feet rested gratefully in the stirrups as he settled himself for a risky ride beneath a small and setting moon down the twenty-two miles to Tampa.

At Fort Brooke the sun had slipped from sight across the bay leaving a sunset sky like a madman's rainbow with the offshore breeze stirring lines through the golden soup of water. Word was brought that a ship was entering the bay some ten miles to the southwest.[37] Soldiers and civilians hurried to the wharf just west of the fort. Major Mountfort with his company had been long and anxiously awaited and

36. "Registers of Enlistment," roll 19.
37. Belton to Jones, January 1, 1836.

hopes ran high that if he could dock without too great a delay he and his men could still overtake and reinforce Major Dade. But minutes became hours and sunset slipped into the envelope of night and still no signal light could be seen from the oncoming ship. Rumors generated by alternate hope and fear made the rounds and impatience grew.

By midnight Captain Belton was feeling the weight of his responsibility. He had been completely confident on the eleventh of December when he had arrived from Fort Morgan, Alabama, with his company,[38] prepared to assume the command from Captain U. S. Fraser. He had been surprised at the concern felt by that officer and subsequently by nearly everyone else in the fort. Since the first of the month Fraser had had all able-bodied men working constantly erecting defenses against what he had assured Captain Belton was imminent attack by the hostile Indians. At first Belton had discounted the danger, writing that "an attack . . . must fail, and by such a result materially aid the interests of the government."[39] But now he had grave doubts. During his two weeks in command, hit-and-run raids in the vicinity of the fort had become commonplace; recently the home of Mr. Simmons, the planter, had been burned and his crops destroyed.[40] West, across the river, some five hundred supposedly friendly Indians were encamped.[41] They had promised to lend their support in case of attack, but it was hard to tell just where you stood with these Seminoles. If they were to be believed, then they had every reason to come to the assistance of the military if the need arose, but on the other hand if the Indians spoke the truth, then he should never have allowed the command to leave.

The chief of those Seminoles who had gone into camp

38. Belton to Jones, December 12, 1835, *FTP*, XXV, 210-11.
39. *Ibid.*, p. 211.
40. *Ibid.*
41. Boyd, *Florida Aflame*, pp. 85-86.

near the fort in early December was Holata Emathla, and he had brought the news of the murder of his brother Charley Emathla. With Holata were over four hundred men, women, and children, in addition to the chiefs of seven bands, declaring themselves prepared to leave in the government ships whenever they should finally arrive. Satisfaction at this defection of a part of the tribe from Osceola was tempered by rumors that a council had been held back in October in the Big Swamp by members of the associated tribes and that a decision had been made approving and adopting as the policy of the Nation the hostile attitude of the Mikasuki tribe and the penalty for agreement to emigration was death.[42] Charley Emathla had been the first man executed.

General Thompson had arranged for a sale of the Indians' cattle to be held on the first day of December, and pens had been constructed to house the animals near Fort King.[43] In spite of the supposed edict, Charley Emathla, weary of struggling, had given up the fight in the hope that by capitulation he might buy peace. He had driven his herd to the fort on November 26 and turned them over to Colonel Yancey, one of the commissioners appointed to appraise their value. Then, with his three daughters, he had set out for home. Along the trail, near the fort, Osceola and a party of Mikasukis had lain in wait. This would be the turning point for most of the tribes. If one traitor delivered himself to the enemy and lived, then the timid would follow. The only faint hope for victory against the white invaders lay with a united front. The peace-loving Emathla had been moving along the trail when suddenly Osceola stood before him. He understood. Without a pause he charged at the young warrior. Osceola fired and simultaneously the crash of other rifles roared out in the quiet of the woods and Charley Emathla was knocked off his feet by nine rounds in his body. The attackers faded into the

42. *Ibid.*, p. 56; Boyd, "Osceola," p. 276.
43. Fanning to Clinch, November 27, 1835, *FTP*, XXV, 200.

palmetto and scrub and three girls were left alone with
their father's corpse.[44]

Word of the murder spread quickly. The six chiefs of
the Nation who were committed to emigration fled precipi-
tantly to Tampa, herding their people and leaving behind
food, clothing, and cattle, to huddle together across the river
from the fort and await the government transports to remove
them from the wrath of the implacable Osceola.

So now they were Captain Belton's problem, along with
two companies of soldiers, half of them on sick report
with fevers and inflammatory diseases.[45] And worse yet, there
were the settlers with their belongings camped on top of
them and complaining bitterly about inadequate protection,
plus an equal number of women and children all worried
sick about their men on the road to Fort King—and all he
could do was wait and sweat. Where the hell could Mountfort be with his reinforcements for Dade? At the most it was
twenty-five miles from the gulf to the fort, and it was hours
since a runner had come in with word that a ship had been
seen swinging across the bar into the bay. He was too tired
to think and too worried to sleep and though it was nearly
midnight, he could see lanterns bobbing about the compound like so many fireflies—dark shadows beneath them
moving endlessly like ants along invisible lines of force,
meeting, pausing in little clusters and moving on, and he
knew they were nursing hope of reinforcements with rumors
and he was grateful that the darkness hid the anxious look
in every face.

Suddenly the alarm was sounding—someone was approaching on the Fort King Road. One of the civilians who
had formed a mounted organization of rangers to patrol the
approaches to the fort[46] shouted for the gate to open—there
was a courier from Dade! The exhausted soldier was brought

44. Wiley Thompson to the Public, November 30, 1835, in Cohen, pp. 67-68;
Fanning to Clinch, November 28, 1835, *FTP*, XXV, 203; Boyd, "Osceola," pp.
277-78.
45. Belton to Jones, December 12, 1835, *FTP*, XXV, 211.
46. *Ibid.*

into the commanding officer's quarters and in the warmth and security of civilized surroundings, Private Jewell did his best to answer the questions put to him by Belton and his staff.

He was from Captain Gardiner's C Company, yes sir, and he'd marched fifteen miles with the command today and left them at the Big Hillsborough where the bridge was burned. No, they'd seen no Indians, but there was plenty of sign and the major was keeping out flankers and entrenching every night. Since the bridge was out, though, they'd have to ford the river and that would slow them down, and the major wanted to know if Major Mountfort was on the way and also the extra rations and ammunition? And sir, could he sleep now?

The knowledge that everything was all right so far was like a dose of laudanum and brows tight with frowns of worry gave way to sighs of relief, but not for long. Indian warfare was a minute-by-minute affair and since Jewell had left them their situation could have changed—they might be in grave danger any time from now on. Belton pushed back the thought long enough to send word to Lieutenant Basinger's lady and the wives of the enlisted men that their husbands were all right—they had encountered no trouble and were safe in camp. It was Christmas Eve, and the best he could do.

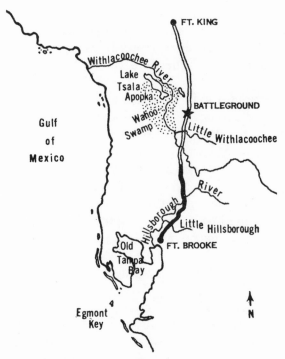

THE THIRD DAY

Friday, December 25, 1835

I T WAS an hour past midnight when Captain Belton, writing hurriedly by the light of a tallow candle, scratched out a note to Major Mountfort and the imperative burden of his words was—hurry! He summoned an Indian runner from the camp across the river and gave him orders to follow the east side of the bay south until he sighted the transport and get this message out to her as fast as he could.[1]

Word had been brought only moments before that the transport carrying Mountfort and his men had been sighted by one of the lookouts stationed far down the bay, but it would be dawn before the runner could reach him. With luck, his ship might drop anchor by noon and there would

1. Belton to Jones, January 1, 1836.

still be time to get on the road. If Dade was delayed by a day at the Big Hillsborough, as seemed likely, Mountfort and his men could overtake the command by a forced march. Yes, the prospects weren't too bad.

He snuffed out the candle and went to bed. In the darkness he lay thinking of the prospects of his most immediate responsibility: those people, military and civilian, who occupied Fort Brooke. They should be reasonably secure within the pickets and with their exposed back open only to the sea, but if anything went wrong—if the Seminoles across the river should change their minds—then he would have his hands full fighting off several hundred warriors with inadequate forces and a scanty supply of ammunition.[2] Provisions were none too abundant, and Holata Emathla's people were living on reduced government rations. It wouldn't take a lot to make them change their minds as to whose side they were on, being forced to sit in their camp exposed as they were to murderous attack by their erstwhile leader and treated like beggars by the government that had always promised so much and done so little.

Two days ago, the evening before Dade set out, there had been a bad upset in Emathla's camp when three Indians of the Tallahassee tribe arrived out of the night bringing a supposedly peaceful talk from Micanopy.[3] They had immediately met in council with Emathla's warriors and Belton had felt it necessary to take them prisoner, for it was almost a certainty that they were spies or had come to assassinate Holata Emathla who had been hunted by Osceola's men since his brother's death. Old Micanopy had no good words for Emathla and the less his messengers said of their "peaceful talk," the better.

It was some comfort to recall Dade's attitude in the conference that had been held later that same night with Emathla. Dade had seemed to think that Abraham would have a salutary effect on Micanopy, and he had expressed

2. Belton to Clinch, December 22, 1835.
3. Belton to Jones, January 1, 1836.

great faith in the Indian character. Dade had dealt with the Seminoles off and on for years, and his opinion was not to be lightly dismissed. Still it had seemed the best course to detain as hostages two of the messengers and send the other, the youngest and best runner, to Fort King with messages for General Clinch and General Thompson, giving the situation here and the numbers and plans of the command that was being sent to the aid of these at Fort King. As a precaution against betrayal by the courier he had written the numbers and other details in French. Whether the messages got through or not, Dade was confident of the success of the mission—and he was in charge.

By morning the wind had shifted to the southeast and the smell of rain was in the air. Through the night Mountfort's transport had been beating into the wind, heading directly northeast up the bay proper toward Fort Brooke. The bay was shaped like an inverted boot, the top of the upper open to the Gulf and the bottom or north end split into two parts corresponding to the toe and heel. The heel, being the deeper of the two, was the site of the fort and the wharf along its edge had been busy since early dawn when the cry "Sail ho" had rung out across the compound. The sentinel on the lookout, sixty feet up in a giant hickory near the shore, had clear view some fifteen miles down the bay.[4] Telescopes were passed from hand to hand as eager eyes watched for a glimpse of the sail that would mean the first of the reinforcements were at hand. The gray morning passed slowly as the transport approached and it was nearly noon before she hove-to several miles off the fort. Here the channel was safely deep and now smaller boats ferried the major and his strong company across the shallow water to the wharf.[5] A holiday-like mood prevailed as the men joined the forces already at the fort. It seemed sure that Dade would soon be reinforced and relatively secure while

4. McCall, p. 200.
5. Belton to Jones, January 1, 1836.

more troops soon due would put to rest any fears for the safety of the fort and its women and children.

Major Mountfort reported to Captain Belton that the transport with Captain Legate's company, under Lieutenant Greyson, should be in shortly and that his company numbered nearly its full strength of fifty men. Most of the baggage for his own company had been sent on the other transport, but since Greyson had not been more than a half-day behind they could soon be fitted out. Belton ordered that they go as far as possible with the necessary preparations in order to be ready to move out by morning, well-fed and rested in an all-out effort to overtake Dade.[6] The bustle of activity helped still more to lift the gloom as Belton's own company and the men of Major Richard Augustus Zantzinger's turned to help the departing men check out what little equipment they had with them. Before dark everything was in readiness for the forced march. The cooks had prepared a Christmas dinner of the best available and the men had proposed heartfelt toasts to the success of all concerned. An almost desperate bond of fellowship seemed to unite the disparate company and personal concern was lost as settlers and soldiers pledged their common Christian heritage.

But the courier, Private Aaron Jewell, was not with them. Long before dark he had ridden out through the gate into the coming night, headed once more northeast up the Fort King Road. The voices and the sounds of Fort Brooke grew fainter through the rain and his horse's hooves pounded steadily on the packed sand. Up there by the river were the captain and thirty-three men of his company, and it was only right that a man should be with friends on Christmas Day.

That morning Dr. Gatlin of Dade's command had crossed to the north bank of the Big Hillsborough River as the line officers readied the troops for crossing. He didn't consider

6. *Ibid.*

it much of a river compared to the goodly Neuse which
flowed near his family's home in Kinston, North Carolina.
There were few things he'd found that really compared
favorably with Kinston and its environs.[7] His grandfather
had been the first governor of the state after the Revolution
and his family had grown accustomed to holding a place of
prominence in the area. The Gatlin children had been
raised in the knowledge that their family line extended
back to the fifteenth century, numbering soldiers, statesmen,
and high public servants among its members. His older
brother Dick had graduated from the Military Academy
in 1832 and was beginning what promised to be a long and
distinguished career with the army, while he, in his early
twenties, was already an assistant surgeon. It was true that
his luck hadn't been too good since receiving his own commission last year, but maybe things were taking a turn for
the better now that he had finally gotten to Florida, the
place he had tried for ever since putting on a uniform.

First there'd been Fort Gibson, a terrible outpost on the
frontier made up of log huts where no civilized man could
happily serve. As he had put it in applying for transfer,
"you will confer a great favor [on] one who does not wish
to stand still in the world . . . by appointing me to . . .
my preference of stations—anywhere south rather than
west—but should prefer Florida for its climate. . . ."[8] That
had been in November and it had still been four months
before he got as far as Fort Jackson, Louisiana, where he
had taken one look around and applied for transfer the day
he arrived. The surgeon general in Washington, Dr. Joseph
Lovell, couldn't seem to get it through his head that a
gentleman of education did not enter the service of his
country in order to tend fever-ridden soldiers at bleak
outposts, miles from the company of gentlemen—not to
mention ladies—where a doctor spent as much time suffer-

7. Gatlin file, N.A.R.S.
8. Gatlin to (presumably) Surgeon General J. Lovell, November 30, 1834,
Gatlin file.

ing from dysentery and fever as he did in treating these same disorders in others. A transfer to some post anywhere along the Atlantic coast as long as it was south of New York would be more suitable though ". . . I am particularly anxious to get to Florida . . . anywhere in the region I have mentioned rather than a confined and unhealthy place like this."[9]

By late summer he finally reached Fort Pickens in Florida situated on an island outside Pensacola Bay with sick troopers and sea gulls for company. This was less to his liking than Fort Jackson. "This post and Fort Jackson," he wrote, "are little better than places of Exile, where a man is almost as much confined, as if he were on a rock in the ocean—the abode of melancholy."[10]

Perhaps it was just the season, though the feeling of depression was hard to cast off as he watched an officer on horseback crossing the river alongside the tall trestles of the burned-out bridge, probing with a long pole for the shallows and picking the best path for the men afoot.[11] It wasn't the discomfort of the light rain or the risk in this whole venture but a combination of things. Mostly it was the melancholy that had been his dour companion for as long as he could remember, made worse by debility brought on by the posts at which he had had to serve. He had always found riding the best antidote for gloom, yet for the past nine months there had been no place where a man could swing into a saddle and race the wind, the pounding and the speed dispelling the mists of melancholy for a time. At home in Kinston it had seemed that a change of scene and habits might put the demon to flight for all time, but he had found it at every post and now here on the Fort King Road.

The thought that this was Christmas morning only fas-

9. Gatlin to Lovell, April 1, 1835.
10. *Ibid.*, September 12, 1835.
11. This method of crossing is described by Lieutenant James Duncan in his diary entry for February 18, 1836, at the crossing of the Big Withlacoochee River. It seems an obvious and reasonable method and I have assumed that Dade's command would have crossed in the same manner.

tened the mood more firmly, for Kinston would be banked
in snow today and the gay bells of carriages would ring in
the streets. In cozy rooms warm-lit by open fires, fond
parents and firm friends would exchange the season's greet-
ings. He could picture his mother and father by a festive
board burdened with the good things of the season, the
Negroes bustling about with drinks and happy laughter
at the least excuse, sister Sarah, only twenty-one and happy
with her first Christmas since her marriage, and sister Mary
swishing about in a new and lovely gown. Perhaps even
Dick was there—on leave from his company and handsome
in his uniform.

John Gatlin stared through eyes misted with rain as the
horses of Dade, Gardiner, and the rest snorted and pawed
near him, cold water dripping in narrowing streams from
their great dark bellies into the white sand and back down
the steep bank where the first of the foot soldiers, muskets
held high, struggled from the swift current. Cursing, lips
blue with the cold, and teeth clenched to keep them from
chattering, the men clambered up the precipitous bank
and out into the gloom of live oaks and brown grass ahead
to take up roving stations as advance guard and prevent
surprise attack while the position of the command was most
vulnerable. Still the men came on, gingerly at first as they
edged reluctantly into the clear, icy water, urged on by
those behind them and by the insistent shouted commands
of the noncommissioned officers. Alternately gasping and
holding their breath they felt their way down the opposite
slope, pale blue trousers sinking deeper and deeper into
fifty-degree water, heavy coats rolled into packs pulled high
on hunched shoulders and only shirts and suspenders still
dry. The water reached to loin height with the ache of a
raw wound, then waist and shirt were under and still the
bottom angled gently down. Little George Herlyhigh, only
five feet two, was almost neck deep before his numb, boot-
clad feet felt the bottom flatten and then start the rise to
the north bank. From the river center the wide-spaced

column gained speed as the men passed the worst the water could do and hurried toward the shore, eager for the dry road where they could empty their boots and wring out their shirts.

A hastily constructed raft was floated out from the far side. It was made of pine logs lashed with rope and big enough to hold a thousand pounds of cannon. The men might wade, but the six-pounder would ride. Now the gun was trundled down the bank, held back with other ropes and with straining men leaning against the weight. With some difficulty it was horsed aboard the raft which now appeared none too large as it tilted dangerously with the weight of the weapon and was steadied by men in the water on both sides. It was shifted carefully until the raft, though low in the water, was riding evenly. Ropes were paid out across the river to ready hands on the north bank, and slowly, trailing ropes still held on the south bank, the raft and its load were pulled out from the shore and into the current. Quickly then, but with care, the raft was towed across, swinging gradually downstream as the current pulled at it, then completing a shallow arc as it reached the north bank. Ropes were made fast to axle and limber and pressure applied from artillerymen on the slope, rolling the cannon slowly off the raft. Moved from center, the shift of weight was unexpectedly great—the disproportion lifted the far edge even more—and with a splash and gurgle the little gun slid from the raft, fell between raft and shore, and rolled from sight in five feet of water, accompanied by unavailing shouts and curses.

Private John Thomas was standing near the spot where the cannon sank. He and others nearby grabbed the ropes that disappeared into the water where the weapon rested just below the surface. The twelve-foot bank was steep— bad enough for horses and men to clamber up while relatively unencumbered, but this would be a real task—towing a thousand-pound dead weight from the suction of the sandy river bottom and up a rutted and irregular bank to the top.

For artillerymen there was no security like that reposing in a wheeled weapon, and with this prize piece out of commission they felt naked and uneasy. Eager hands grasped the ropes with Thomas and pulled, first in disorder and then together. Reluctantly the river yielded to their combined efforts and the trail of the limber and the high wheels reappeared, clods of blue clay and white sand clinging to the dripping spokes, then sliding back to rush down in the current like cloudy banners. But initial strength faded quickly against the tremendous weight, and Thomas, strain as he might, felt the gradual motion slow, and then stop. More men were jumping and sliding down the bank, wet boots coated with sand like filings on a magnet, to squeeze between the others for a hand on the ropes. To the mingled commands of both officers and noncoms, they pulled and heaved together.

Thomas stood with one leg extended down-slope and braced in the sand, the other nearly doubled under his body in a half-crouch, arms reaching down and the small of his back the fulcrum on which the weight was carried. Suddenly he felt a stab of pain so unexpected and so great that a gasp that was almost a scream burst between his clenched teeth. Releasing the rope, he stumbled stiffly away from the line to fall, moaning, on the sand.[12]

12. This incident is based upon a Surgeon's Certificate for Pension included in the Thomas file, N.A.R.S., which states: "on the 25th day of December . . . at . . . the big Hillsborough River . . . Thomas . . . was injured in his back while assisting to lift a six pounder out of the . . . river." While lending detail to this particular phase of the march, this report seemed (to the author) to explain finally, one of the questions long hanging over the "Dade Massacre," as expressed in Boyd, *Florida Aflame*, p. 90: "on the afternoon of the 29th, a date hardly credible considering the distance to have been covered . . . Thomas . . . returned to the fort. . . ." The "distance" referred to, of course, is from the battleground of the 28th to Fort Brooke, or slightly more than sixty miles, truly a remarkable journey in twenty-four hours for a wounded man to cover on foot. The fact seems to be, however, that Thomas was not in the battle—did not in fact go any farther from the fort than the Hillsborough River, from whence he was sent back with an injury serious enough to cause his discharge in June, 1837. Other details of his condition will be discussed as they occur.

As to the details of the crossing, they have been reconstructed on the following basis (lest the reader assume that we have slipped from history into fiction); first, the surgeon's certificate indicates that the cannon *was*, somehow, *in the*

Dr. Gatlin, watching from the bluff above, quickly dismounted and sent men down the bank to bring up the tall, blond trooper. On the grass alongside the road, out of the way of action, Dr. Gatlin observed that the soldier maintained nearly the motionlessness of death, though his eyes were wide and he was obviously conscious. He lay a little on one side, knees flexed slightly and fingers stretched claw-like into the tufted weeds as though to hold himself away from the ground. To judge by the whispered groans and stentorious breathing, the blanched look of an already pale complexion, the injured man was suffering intense pain.

Even before he made an examination, he knew what had happened. In his eagerness, the soldier had placed too great a strain on what was probably an already weakened back, and a wafer-like disc in his spine was crushed, pinching nerves that produced unbearable pain. Neither his training at medical college nor his service in apprenticeship had prepared John Gatlin for a positive course of treatment for this Achilles' heel of the human race. Back in civilization he would have prescribed bed rest—weeks of it in this case— and mild doses of laudanum while the pain was at its worst, but here there was no bed, no rest, and no laudanum. He did what he could to make the man comfortable, then reported to the major.[13]

Already delayed by the burned bridge, depressed by the

---

river (since Thomas was assisting to lift it out). Assuming that it *fell* there, it had to fall *from* something and a raft constructed on the site would seem to be that something. A raft, heavily laden, would have to be towed across the river and ropes would be both simple and available. As to the depth of water, temperature, and the slope of the banks, the author will attest to the relative accuracy of these from personal experience and a study of old and new survey records.

With reference to the scene as a whole, we have *not* found as detailed a description at the time as we have presented. However, the known facts, treated with reason and common sense, seem to indicate that the event, as reconstructed here, is relatively accurate.

13. Without meaning to become unnecessarily personal, the author would like to offer in support of the validity of Thomas' condition here the fact of his own encounter with a similar back injury requiring months of immobility and finally surgery. In addition, discussion with medical persons indicate that these symptoms are relatively typical of the condition.

rain, and irritated by the accident to the six-pounder, Major Dade had only one choice in the case of Private Thomas. In Gatlin's opinion the man couldn't stand the journey of eighty miles stretched in a wagon, jolting over every root and rock from here to Fort King; he would have to return him to Fort Brooke. The already inadequate size of the command precluded the possibility of detailing a guard for him and certainly he couldn't mount a horse even if there were one to spare. No, Thomas would have to return alone —on foot. They could ferry him back over the river by raft, but that was it. They had lost too much time already and must get on the road.

Within the hour the little command had completed the crossing, the cannon finally up the hill and wiped as dry as possible, the supply wagon floated and pulled across, the troops once more in double file with flankers out and advance guard leading the way. From across the river John Thomas watched them disappear in the rain-shrouded woods. Dr. Gatlin had said the pain would abate somewhat if he were still for several hours and he lay unmoving—in his haversack some meat and bread, his musket lying near to hand, in his pocket six dollars, and overall the pain.

Gatlin rode in silence and dismal mood through rain that came and went from a soggy sky. Thomas had been the first accident—how many more would there be? How many men would be down before this march was over? He hated to think of the soldier left by the river alone and injured, but there was nothing more he could do for him and it was just one of the drawbacks in a business that had more than its share. He had thought that each of his former posts had been a low point—from bleak frontier to lonely island—but surely this was as bad as a man could find. It was difficult to believe that he had actually *requested* transfer to Florida, but then who would have thought that he would be sent to a place like Fort Brooke where even the mail came only once a month?[14] Why not Pensacola

14. Gatlin to Lovell, November 20, 1835.

where there was at least a pure atmosphere and the enjoyments of society could be had instead of isolated Fort Pickens and Fort Brooke? Key West would not have been so bad, or better yet, Fort Macon or even Beaufort in his own North Carolina. The latter place "has no chance for any man in the service but myself, being but seventy miles from my home."[15] And Dr. Lovell had given him reason to think that he might be transferred there by the end of winter.

Miserable and wet, it was hard to remember why he had ever volunteered in the first place. Certainly the pay had not been a great inducement to compensate for this type of service. As assistant surgeon, a doctor's rank was equivalent to no less than a first lieutenant and no more than a captain, with the monthly pay of thirty dollars plus twenty-four dollars for subsistence. In any southern station it took a man's entire pay to cover board, lodging, and washing, leaving only twenty-four to buy his clothing and provide him with the incidentals, not to mention putting a little away for his old age.[16] Gatlin jumped his horse over a narrow creek that cut the road. At least he was spared the necessity of walking like the foot soldiers who slogged on through sand and mud in wet boots and sodden clothing. For even these small favors he was grateful now.

North of the river the road continued straight mile after mile. The map showed no rivers to cross, no hills to climb or avoid—only open pine barrens similar to yesterday's, but on land a little higher and with fewer ponds and swamps. Barring accident or misadventure they should be able to reach the hilly land near a lake of some size about a dozen miles ahead before making camp, perhaps even make a few miles beyond it. By fording they had saved precious time and the sun was not yet well into the sky, hidden still behind the overcast; already the shaggy cypress growth that bordered the river was nearly lost in the haze of slow falling

15. *Ibid.*, November 12, 1835.
16. Motte, Introduction, p. xv.

rain. The tall gray cypress, barren now of fern-like foliage, had given way to stands of scrub short-leaf yellow pine sprung from sandy soil and alternate areas of hammock land, rich in humus and forested with hardwoods—ash, maple, and gum.

By the third mile they had reached the green saw-toothed palmetto, a sure sign of rising ground, for the "little palm" would not grow in wet ground. Branching even farther away to the right, or northeast, was the swift-flowing Hillsborough marked by the cypress-studded flood land that bordered it. To the left and paralleling the road in a meandering line of least resistance flowed a small, narrow stream, a feeder of the main river, nursing from its meager flow the clustered small trees and thick brush that could give an Indian perfect concealment. These rivers and the full reach of the flood lands that extended in some cases for miles beyond the banks were the natural traps of the Seminole. As adaptable as pond birds to the wet and snake-ridden deeps of the swamp, they could strike with deadly effect in this kind of country and be gone before the full realization of danger became apparent to a white man. But the splash and curse of flankers well out on each side of the column should give a fair measure of security.

In these dry winter months the road was well drained as it swung along through the flat open country that was growing steadily broader. On the flanks, the guards had to fight and struggle through virgin swamp and wood, all the while watching for the first sign of Indian attack. An almost imperceptible rise of ground since they had left the river was fast thinning the dense stands of willow, ash, and sweet gum and giving a clearer view through the rain-fogged morning across the palmetto tops and toward the low hills ahead.

Between the Big Hillsborough and the Big Withlacoochee Rivers the trail would gradually climb for a dozen miles until it reached an elevation over a hundred feet higher than the river banks, crossing great sand hills where groves

of wild, bitter-sweet oranges crowned the hills—a difficult
and exhausting trail where toes and calf muscles would soon
ache with the effort of trying to gain solid purchase. Then
would come the easier miles down and through the thick-
ening yellow pine forests to the lowland and swamp to the
Withlacoochee crossing. After that, sixty more miles of level
ground to Fort King.

With the thinning of the water-nourished thickets and
scrubs the column entered the first of the foothills. The
underbrush had nearly disappeared now; the low green sea
of palmetto blanketed the earth. The hardwoods were left
behind and in this higher ground they entered vast stands
of enormous yellow pine, straight limbless trunks towering
more than a hundred feet above the rustling wet palmetto
and the dense thickets of blackjack oak.

To Edwin De Courcy and other Englishmen who plodded past them the name was familiar, for the black bark
resembled the big tar-impregnated leather drinking vessels
called blackjacks, still in use in many parts of England.[17]
But there was no stout English ale here, or Irish whiskey
for that matter—only Cuban rum in a keg on the supply
wagon and damn little of that.

Another mile and they could make out a dwelling on the
right, some five hundred feet off the road. A settler's crude
cabin[18] abandoned by the Indian threat, to judge by the
absence of smoke that should have been rising from a cook
fire. The turned field to the north had been painfully
cleared and planted but hardy winter weeds were all that
thrived there now in the absence of man.

All through the day Dade and his men pushed on due
north, their progress interrupted only by short rest periods
and a midday halt to eat. From morning to night they would
vary only a half-mile off a north course where the road
swung out to avoid a large pond and then a lake. But they

17. *True,* October, 1964, p. 57.
18. Original government survey of township 26S, range 21E, section 4, plat
and field notes.

had only traded the ankle-twisting clumps of yesterday's swamp grass for the nightmare quality of loose sand. They should be safer from attack on the slopes of the endless hills of sand for the land was high and clear of ground cover and from neighboring hills the flankers could watch for hostiles, though the sand had become an enemy in itself. Leg muscles softened by garrison duty had been initiated by yesterday's long march; this morning men had hobbled around the encampment like cripples while aching legs were forced to stretch and loosen. Now, as the hours and the hills passed, men were afraid to get off their feet during a break for fear their legs would tighten and cramp, for this was not a time when a man would care to drop behind. They were away from the swamp and moving always deeper into the heart of the Nation. The feeling was strong that they moved under the eyes of the Seminoles. Old Indian fields had been passed, and in the hills during the afternoon they had seen an Indian town apparently deserted.[19] So far they had crossed relatively uninhabited country, but this was the edge of territory that was as much home to the Seminole people as anything that existed. The banks of the Withlacoochee River which would cross their route fifteen miles ahead abounded in their towns and villages and they traveled the river in dugout cypress canoes from its source to the gulf.[20] They had roamed these hills for generations in search of deer, bear, and turkey, and the prolific groves of wild oranges had become a staple in their diet. At the edge of a grove could still be seen the trees felled with tomahawks by passing Indian families who would camp for a week at a time and eat nothing but the fruit of the fallen tree.[21] This was the real beginning of the shrunken Seminole Nation and a man

19. Duncan diary, entry for February 17, 1836.
20. Particularly indicative of Indian settlement in this area is a survey along the river made by Lieutenant John Fitzgerald Lee in 1837, and covering letter (Lee to Lieutenant I. A. Chamber, May 12, 1837) found in General Information Index, Records of the Office of the Adjutant General, National Archives, Record Group 94.
21. McCall, p. 196.

was a fool who thought they would not fight for it. Sobering thoughts were marshaled to combat the urge to stop—to rest —for a man who dropped out might not come back.

Captain Upton S. Fraser was uneasy in his role as field commander of Company B, Third Artillery. He had spent twenty-one years coming up through the ranks from ensign and probably more than any other man in the command he doubted the wisdom of their mission. Determined to give no sign of concern, he often rode apart from the command, taking small parties with him, impressing the men with his cheerful, confident mood, but scouring carefully the woods and hammocks sometimes for a mile or more off.[22] It was preposterous that this handful should try to force its way through an aroused country that numbered over five thousand Indians to whom this little command represented the advance guard of an invading horde. Their one chance, Fraser thought, and it was a weak one, lay in the hope that Mountfort was on the way. He caught himself again and again listening for the shout from the rear guard that would mean that Mountfort's advance guard had been sighted, though there was really little chance of it now. After last night when Seminoles had been unmistakably heard beyond the bivouac, boldly shouting so the white men would know that they were there beyond the firelight, it seemed to Fraser that only a miracle would see them through, and perhaps Mountfort and his command *were* that miracle. Double their number would still be a great deal less than safe, but Indians had been bluffed before and two hundred armed and disciplined soldiers would give pause to twice that many Seminoles. And even to himself he had to admit that, once away from Fort Brooke, Dade had had no choice except to do what they were doing. If this was an Indian trap, turning back would only spring it while pushing on might awe the Indians by its boldness. They admired courage and certainly to those whom he felt sure were watching their every move, this tiny band marching seemingly unafraid and confident

22. "Personal Reminiscences," p. 72.

must give them pause to wonder. He rode silently on, absorbed in his thoughts, and those that rode near may have noticed that he seemed always to be listening for a sound that never came.

And just beyond the nearby hills, a Seminole scout lay watching and listening too. Since the troops left Tampa Bay they had been watched over faithfully. Scouts preceded, paralleled, and followed with the skill and deftness of experts—which they were. And no longer was each brave acting individually. This, too, they had learned from the white men. Throughout the day they shadowed the column but offered no interference, as Osceola had ordered, and each night a runner was sent to the camp of the subchief to report the progress of the command and their position for the night. The hate and determination of Osceola had been a thing of wonder and now so great had his power grown that none dared disobey. Not a shot was to be fired until he gave the word.

In council it had been decided that some blow must be struck and true to the agreement of last April the tribes had been assembling—but to fight for the country, not to leave it. With fanatical singleness of purpose Osceola had determined that foremost for him was a settling of accounts at Fort King, then he would return to the Wahoo Swamp to join the main body for a possible attack on the two companies marching through the Nation to the north.[23] He had said *"General Thompson is my friend, I shall see to him,"* and he would.[24]

He left the Swamp two days' march ahead of the troops who had slept last night on the bank of the Lockcha Popka Chiska, or Hillsborough, as the white men called it.[25] By morning he could be in position outside Fort King and there he could wait patiently for his "good friend," pay his long-overdue debt, and return. The troops could wait.

23. Statement by Alligator as reported by Sprague, p. 90.
24. *Ibid.*, p. 90.
25. McCall, p. 189.

Private Aaron Jewell, en route from Fort Brooke to rejoin his command, had been in the saddle since late afternoon.[26] He didn't force his mount for he still had a long ride ahead. Night had fallen before he forded the Hillsborough and the high quarter moon was obscured by the vault of moss-shrouded oak limbs, leaving the water black and seemingly shoreless. But his comrades had evidently forded since the bridge still hung above, a broken thing, and there were only cold ashes of the fires that had flared so cheerfully the night before within their entrenchment. If they crossed early this morning they must be a good ten miles up the road by now and he would do well to overtake them as soon as possible if he expected to get any sleep before they moved on in the morning.

Beyond the ford he left the crowding river growth and the road shone forth, a wide path of rutted sand in the pale light. In the back of his mind there lurked the thought that this was not quite real—a Yankee farmer had no business riding like Paul Revere through the Florida moonlight with official letters in his saddlebags and five thousand wild Indians on the loose somewhere in the night. What the hell was he, Aaron Jewell, doing here? He listened to the hooves of his horse beat a powerful melody and he shied away from the thought of the ears that might be listening. Better to think about his mission—the look the major had given him when he had volunteered back there at the river, the kind things that people at the fort had said about his bravery,

26. The time of Jewell's departure from the fort cannot be determined exactly from available records, but the time given here is based upon Belton's statement of January 1, 1836: "... Jewell ... had left the detachment ... with the news of the burning of Big Hillsboro bridge ... the 2nd day"— December 24. Since Dade reached the bridge in late afternoon, and assuming that he despatched Jewell promptly for Fort Brooke, Jewell should have covered the twenty-five miles in no more than a couple of hours, arriving by early evening. On returning to the command the next day he had an additional distance to travel (a minimum of forty miles) and since Belton states that he rejoined Dade "about 11 o'clock on the night of the [25th] ..." he must have ridden mostly after dark which would have slowed him further. Figuring back then from eleven o'clock, he must have left the fort *after* noon, but *before* night, hence "late afternoon" in the text.

the looks on the faces of his comrades in Company C when he would come in tonight, and their rough jokes and insults to hide their admiration and affection—maybe these were the things that even Paul Revere had felt—the things that made ordinary men climb out of their ruts to do the things that must be done. And then on the practical level perhaps this too would be entered on his service record under "Remarks" to offset that under "Desertion." But right now, as he strained across low and distant hills for sight of a friendly campfire, he'd trade those hopes for safety.

Standing guard in the night, the sentries heard him first. With backs to the low flame that burned within the long protective breastwork, they kept the vigil over sleeping comrades rolled loosely in blankets that made comfortable the faint chill of retreating cold. At first the soft and distant pounding of hooves was barely audible above the combined sounds of men stirring in their sleep, the rustle and snap of a long fire and the lonely, repetitious cry of night hawks in the darkness left by the setting moon. Then straining for the least sound of movement in an alien night it came more clearly—the steady approach of a single horse. From the hills to the south the rider must have seen their light by now and he must be a white man for he came on at a clearly increasing pace. The officer of the day had heard it too and struggling figures were rising from the ground, half-shrouded in blankets, grabbing up muskets and stumbling away from the fire to drop on their knees behind the log barrier. This was no attack—not from the sound of it—but in a place like this a man who wanted to live didn't accept any sound or motion in the night as innocent. Crouching men murmured curses against their own fears, and some who had forgotten prayers remembered, their bearded lips moving in the familiar patterns of childhood.

Then the rider was in the firelight and fear was forgotten in hearty welcome. Like an animated letter from home, Jewell was touched and shaken and made to repeat every tiding from the fort as though it were half a world away and words, still warm, could somehow bring it close. The questions of Major Dade cut through confusion. Jostling quieted while events at Tampa Bay were brought into logical sequence. Disappointment that Major Mountfort was not close behind was lessened with the knowledge that he was at least pulling out in the morning and would bend every effort toward overtaking them and that he brought additional ammunition and rations. And better yet, Lieutenant Greyson with his company should be in by then and would accompany him. Reinforcement would soon be on the way—on the double!

For a time sleep was banished and again men gathered by the fire, kicking it to stir the embers and setting up dancing columns of brilliant sparks that seemed to share their pleasure. Coffee and meat and bread were urged on Jewell by eager, grateful hands and loud voices of mutual encouragement brought relief from the strain of smothered fear. Yet weary muscles and fatigued emotions demanded rest for the day now done and the day ahead and men rested happy, optimistic now for chances which had seemed to glimmer weakly. But here and there a thoughtful soldier lay awake and wondered whether help was any good when it started three days late?

Other men lay sleepless in the night. Major Mountfort needed rest for the march at dawn but unless Greyson's transport was sighted during the night and the supplies brought ashore, there would be no equipment for him and his company—aside from the fact that Greyson's company itself could not join him. If there was uneasiness felt for Fraser's and Gardiner's companies, how much less chance would he and fifty men have alone? The troops were ready and eager to leave and he had seen to it that they were fed well and bedded early in preparation, yet facts had to be faced and for his company it was his task to face them. For perhaps the thousandth time he felt sick with wonder at Greyson's whereabouts. His transport had been close behind on the run from Key West, and yet for the past twelve hours they had been waiting and not even a light had been seen across the reach of Tampa Bay. Well, he must be in by morning.

FT. KING

Withlacoochee River

Lake
Tsala
Apopka

BATTLEGROUND

Wahoo
Swamp

Little Withlacoochee

Gulf
of
Mexico

River

Hillsborough

Little Hillsborough

Old
Tampa
Bay

FT. BROOKE

Egmont
Key

N

THE FOURTH DAY

Saturday, December 26, 1835

T HE BREEZE had held steady from the southeast during
the night, blowing toward the fort across the mangrove
swamps and moving the twenty-four-starred flag in slow
ripples from the top of its tall wooden pole. From pine
boughs far above the steep roofs of wooden barracks, long
pendants of gray moss swayed gracefully and the air was
sweet with the fragrance of yellow jasmine. The sun rose
as bright as hope and there was not a cloud in the sky as
Captain Belton scanned the bay. But down the long reach of
water there was no ship, no sail—no reinforcements. The
fainter the hope of help, the stronger seemed the impulse
to proclaim it. Already a young Indian runner had been
sent north by the Fort King Road with a duplicate of Private

95

Jewell's message—just in case Jewell had not made it through—reassuring Major Dade that help and food and ammunition would soon be on the way.[1]

In the early dawn, having sent the runner off to bolster Dade with hope, Captain Belton could only pace in the privacy of his quarters and wonder, in agonized waiting, where Greyson's transport could be. It was impossible that he could have been attacked by Seminoles with only dugouts—or if he had, that they could not have been easily repelled; equally inconceivable was the possibility of shipwreck—for the sea had been calm with only light rain and little wind, yet he had been close on the wake of Mountfort's ship when he entered the bay on the twenty-fourth. Each round of speculation brought him to the inevitable conclusion that the transport *had* to be tacking cross wind in the channel, or standing well out from the wharf below the fort—but reason each time was brought up short as his telescope searched the ruffled harbor. Only sea gulls hung in the air and only pelicans drifted on the water.

Everything that could be prearranged was ready—Holata Emathla had supplied fifteen warriors to handle an equal number of pack horses loaded with three thousand pounds of rations while a wood wagon and mule cart had been secured to carry the gear for Mountfort's company—but there was no question of his company marching alone.[1a] Unless their supplies arrived aboard the long-awaited transport, they would have to travel without their baggage of arms, ammunition, and equipment. They might as well be naked. He had risked two companies, but gestures would not save them and Mountfort's leaving would be nothing more than that. He regretted having allowed the command to march when there was only the *expectation* of three additional companies for it had been his firm intention to send no less than four together at full

1. Belton to Jones, January 1, 1836.

1a. Belton to Clinch, December 26, 1835, from Records of United States Regular Army Mobile Units, 1821-1920, Record Group 391 (selected pages of Orderly Book, Company B, 2nd United States Artillery, 1834-38).

strength to force their way through to Fort King. Since the twelfth of December when he had written to the adjutant general, confidently predicting that "Three more companies from New Orleans and Key West are daily expected. . . . Two companies of the garrison here, and two of those expected, are by existing orders to be detached to Fort King. . . ."[2] Yet only thirty-nine men under Dade's command had arrived in addition to Major Mountfort's company. Clinch's order for reinforcements had been held in suspension for a week waiting for additional troops, but by the twenty-third, with Dade's arrival, compliance seemed practical and he'd let them go—every man thinking that they were only the vanguard of a larger army-to-be. But now they were a full three days away and there was no army— there was nothing.

Full dawn had come and across the bay there was still no sign of any transport and he knew that Dade and his one hundred would have to make it through alone or not at all.

At the same hour, one hundred and six miles north of Fort Brooke and seventy-one miles beyond Dade's awakening encampment, Osceola lay concealed in a densely grown hammock six hundred yards from the tall palisade walls of Fort King. In front of him, beyond the border of the hammock and surrounded by low-cropped grass stood the log house of Erastus Rogers, the sutler. To the right and left lay comparatively open plain. Scattered about outside the fort were several small structures—the washhouse, bakehouse, and other utility buildings[3]—but to the dedicated eyes of the Seminole, the fort was the center of interest. Within its walls dwelt Wiley Thompson, the man he held responsible for the dire circumstances of his entire people and for his own humiliation. The recollection of his imprisonment in the white man's cage under the eyes of both

2. Belton to Jones, December 12, 1835.
3. Lieutenant Joseph W. Harris to General George Gibson, December 30, 1835, quoted in Boyd, *Florida Aflame*, p. 71; Boyd, "Osceola," p. 280; Sprague, p. 89.

soldiers and Seminoles fed his hatred with steady fuel. The time for settlement had come and above all other accounts this one must be closed.

The protective walls about Fort King dominated the landscape. The fort was set on a slight rise of ground over-looking an undulating pine barren to the south and close by the walls rose a spring, clear and cold. The palisade around the barracks and compound had been constructed from pines that grew in profusion across the entire hammock on which the fort and agency stood. Split in half and with the bark side out, the logs were placed endwise with their bases set deep in the ground and their upper portions rising twenty feet to sharpened points. They were strong and sturdy, snug against one another and braced from the inside with horizontal planks, more susceptible to fire than fire-arms. At each angle of the walls stood a blockhouse and just visible above the high pickets was the gaudy banner that waved from a tall pole.[4]

Between the walls and the protective screen of verdant palmetto the agency office stood alone, almost within the shadow of the high walls a hundred yards away. Here the erstwhile agent carried out his duties, passing frequently between the office and the fort in an area busy with the activities of the more than two hundred troops now sta-tioned there. A few Indians friendly to the whites hung about, but for none of these did Osceola have the dogmatic interest that he had for the agent. Hours passed as he lay concealed watching the activity before him. Scattered throughout the underbrush and the woods to the north, some fifty warriors of the Mikasuki tribe waited under his control.[5] He conceived and discarded many plans, but he was not discouraged and he was not really impatient. When the time was right, as it must be eventually, he would strike.

To the Indians nearly half a mile away the sound of voices raised in command carried clearly from the fort with the

4. "Macomb's Mission to the Seminoles."
5. Boyd, "Osceola," p. 280.

occasional rumble of a drum or the military imperative of a bugle. The sutler and his assistants continued their work of moving goods from his combined home and store into the fort while General Thompson worked in his office.[6] With unflagging attention Osceola lay listening and watching. Beside him in the grass lay his rifle.

Within the walls Colonel Fanning made last minute preparations to move out. In November General Clinch had begun the concentration of troops at Fort Drane, twenty-six miles northwest of Fort King, and Fanning was under orders to take three of the four companies at Fort King to join him there.[7] Fort Drane had been built on Clinch's plantation which included several thousand acres of first-rate land,[8] now a gathering point for all the men the commanding general could muster. The Indian alarms had aroused the populace of the entire Territory and in addition to preparing for the battles that he felt sure would soon be upon them, General Clinch was being called upon to guard and protect scattered frontier settlements.

The troops were glad to be leaving. In the quiet of the past weeks, boredom had settled on the camp and the air was full of the usual complaints. Paymaster Lytle had arrived, but without any pay; food was running low and biscuits were bringing three dollars apiece; perhaps worst of all, a man had to pay up to a dollar for a single drink of whiskey.[9]

Fanning could sympathize with his men but he had bigger worries than the price of liquor. He knew Clinch had counted on his receiving reinforcements from Tampa Bay and had not meant to leave Fort King manned only by a weak company of the Third Artillery under Captain Thomas W. Lendrum.[10] Yet Fanning's concern was at least as great for the men who might be trying to get through to

6. Harris to Gibson, December 30, 1835.
7. *Ibid.*
8. Patrick, p. 61.
9. *Army and Navy Chronicle*, New Series, V, 199.
10. Harris to Gibson, December 30, 1835.

him as for those already here. The fort had strong defensive walls, while George Gardiner would have little protection beyond courage. But for any troops at Fort Brooke, including his brother-in-law, he could do nothing now except "hope that such information as the Commanding Officer at Tampa Bay had of the movements of the enemy in his own neighborhood, would be a sufficient clue to the dangerous state of the whole region for deciding him upon retaining the two companies, and even *all four* when they should have arrived. . . ."[11]

The civilians and troops here should be all right if they followed his orders to sleep within the pickets every night and keep a close guard by day.[12] He could give no guarantees, but if a man wanted guarantees he shouldn't join the army.

The north gates swung open. Colonel Fanning moved out at the head of his troops, taking the road leading west of north past a thick hammock of palmetto. The sound of drums moved with them and the long file left behind a pall of white dust that settled on the fronds.

Osceola saw the haversacks and supply wagon and knew that these men were not planning on returning soon. That left one company and a few civilians to defend the fort, and the gates still stood open. It was clear that patience brought unexpected rewards.

Ten miles south of the Withlacoochee River, Major Dade followed the advance guard through bright and pleasant countryside. It was warmer today and here they should be relatively safe from attack. The road wound only a little and the hills were gentle with the green leaves of live oaks turned half-silver by the morning sun. After yesterday's gray skies and rain and the accident with the gun, the start of this day could only be encouraging with its coffee and

11. ". . . data from the letters of Col. Fanning . . . [plus] a further account received from him in person. . . ." Gardiner file.
12. Harris to Gibson, December 30, 1835.

full bellies before an early start. The jingle of harness seemed to reflect good spirits even in his mount and the major settled in the worn saddle, polished anew by three days of steady use, ready for what the day might bring. The advance guard was moving steadily but not fast, the entire column held to the pace of the scrubby oxen that brought the wagon. Dade could see the major portion of his command strung out behind as they kept in double file within the confines of the roadway, their black caps bobbing in broken rhythm and shepherded along by Basinger, Mudge, Keais, and the other junior officers.

At moments like this, when their chances looked good, it was easy to recall the summer of 1825 when he had brought another command, much like this one, through the same country and against the same sort of odds.[13] Lieutenant George McCall had been with him then and a handful of other officers with another cumbersome six-pounder. Their rations were carried on pack mules instead of a wagon and they had not been cursed with the slow-plodding oxen. The whole trip had been made in five days from Fort Brooke to Fort King. Then as now they had had to ford the three main rivers but it was a different proposition in July than it was in December and this time some of the men were in weakened condition with heavy colds since crossing the Hillsborough and marching all day in wet clothing. Late this afternoon they would be in for it again when they reached the Withlacoochee, but they could make camp just north of the river and dry out before a chill set in. The sun was feeling almost hot as they headed just east of north and the warmth felt good. The return of Jewell had had a good effect on the men and all things seemed to augur well. With that kind of courage, and unfailing caution, they had a good chance.

Courage was something that meant a lot to the major. Private Jewell's volunteering to travel back to the fort and

13. McCall, p. 147; Eloise Robinson Ott and Louis Hickman Chazal, *Ocali Country* (Ocala, Fla., 1966), p. 21; Boyd, *Florida Aflame,* pp. 38-39.

return was something he'd never forget. It was reminiscent of Lieutenant McCall on a long ago day at the Seminole Agency near Fort King.

It was a month after he and McCall had brought their command through to Fort King and Indian unrest had been quieted. A pen had been set up near the agency where government cattle were killed and butchered for Indian consumption. The agent (at that time Mr. Gad Humphreys) had invited the officers to join him and the Indians in trying their marksmanship. A good steer had been selected for Captain Yancey, whose shot only staggered the beast. It stood enraged, blood streaming from a wound below the eye. Lieutenant McCall had then been asked to try his luck with the agent's reloaded rifle. He went over the eight-foot fence and advanced halfway across the pen before he could get the attention of the wounded animal and a fair chance for a forehead shot. Immediately the beast lowered its head and charged while McCall coolly raised his rifle and sighted in on the juggernaut. Almost at the sound of the shot the beast was falling dead at his feet and McCall had not moved. Then a shout from Indians and soldiers along the fence gave warning that another animal had broken from the herd across the pen and was charging down on him. There was no time to reload and little time to reach the safety of the wall. He got to the fence and his foot was on the lower rail with the infuriated beast only yards away when a big Seminole who had sprung to the top reached down and grabbed his arm, swinging him up like an infant just as the onrushing steer crashed into the fence beneath him.

For a moment the Indian held him, his arms around his body and one hand on his chest. He put him down and turned to Humphreys. "His heart is quiet: he was not afraid." [14]

Twenty-two years of military service had covered many such moments along with times of boredom. Since March 29, 1813, when he had received his commission as a

14. McCall, p. 159.

third lieutenant in the Twelfth Infantry at the age of twenty-one, he had done everything from building boats and forts to arresting foreign diplomats and Seminole Indians. It had been a pretty even mixture of pleasant garrison life in comfortable quarters with the rough accommodations of outpost life.

In 1816 he had made first lieutenant and a transfer to the Fourth Infantry. Two years later, in 1818, he received his first assignment in Florida at Fort Barrancas, nine miles southwest of Pensacola on the north bank of Pensacola Harbor,[15] presenting him with the opportunity of contact with civilized society that was often missing from stations near the southern frontier. Eight transfers and three years more brought him back, this time to stand on the Plaza Ferdinand while the Fourth Infantry band played the "Star Spangled Banner" and Spanish and American flags traded places in the official transfer of Florida to the United States. It was a fine moment for a military officer as General Andrew Jackson and Don José Callava, Spanish Governor of West Florida, passed between the parallel and facing ranks of Spanish and American troops, arms raised in salute, and the sultry blue sky carried the booming of a twenty-one gun salute from the sloop of war *Hornet* anchored in the bay.

Every day since Captain Dade had arrived in the city from Montpelier, Alabama, with General Jackson, rain had come sluicing down to wash the sun-baked buildings and bathe the palms and flowers that lined the streets and filled the many gardens, but each day the downpour would end in brilliant sunshine and the city would come alive once more. The picturesque and narrow streets were overhung with wrought iron galleries from which ladies observed the passing scene, and a handsome young officer might make the acquaintance of a great variety of lovely women that passed,

15. This and following references to Dade's assignments through the years are taken from a schedule furnished by N.A.R.S., "Records of the Office of the Adjutant General," Records Group 94, Document File 970418. Information on Fort Barrancas is taken from *United States Military Reservations, National Cemeteries and Military Parks*, p. 55.

silk skirts softly swishing, in the crowds of cutlassed seamen, Spanish soldiers, Jamaican Negroes, and a few Seminoles. It was a different, more sensual atmosphere than that of Tidewater Virginia and one more suited to a young and gallant captain who was also single. And here there were adventures for a soldier that could gain him both position and recognition, essential for a man with ambition. In August, 1821, General Jackson, now governor of the new Territory, sent Dade with a squad of men to arrest Don Callava, lately governor for Spain, as a result of some difficulty over the surrender of papers on the latter's part. This was a move of possible international proportions, but the arrest was made and the indignant Callava placed in the city jail for a day or two. Happily the affair was settled in spite of a somewhat liberal interpretation of his own powers by Jackson and serious trouble was averted. The excitement of the event was a tonic to the garrison of American forces for whom boredom and stagnation were the real enemy. Dade's part in the business could be rated as an advantage to him for he was becoming known to those in authority, from Lieutenant Colonel George Brooke, in command of the Fourth Regiment, to General Jackson, hero of New Orleans.[16]

By the first of the year he was in Baton Rouge, Louisiana, as a member of the General Court-Martial for one month, then back in Pensacola until autumn. For the next few years he carried out routine military chores, principally recruiting, and by May, 1823, received a six-month furlough followed by sick leave at his home in Virginia. Then it was back to recruiting until January of 1824, when, with Colonel Brooke, Lieutenant McCall, a few other officers, and four companies of the Fourth Infantry, he boarded the brig *William and Henry* bound for Tampa Bay.[17]

The Treaty of Moultrie Creek had called for the Indians

16. Marquis James, *The Life of Andrew Jackson* (New York, The Bobbs-Merrill Co., 1938), pp. 313-14, 323-25.

17. Brooke to Major General Jacob Brown, February 5, 1824, quoted in Grismer, pp. 56-58; Boyd, *Florida Aflame*, p. 30.

to be confined to the heart of the Territory, an area running one hundred and twenty-five miles north and south by seventy-five east and west, and isolated from each coast by at least twenty miles, a position that would insure their eventually being entirely surrounded by white men.[18] Colonel James Gadsden, United States Army engineer, a commissioner of the Moultrie Creek Treaty and architect of the Treaty at Payne's Landing, was commissioned to survey the boundaries of the reservation and wrote to Colonel Brooke at the end of the year. "The Indians have of late exhibited something like an unfriendly feeling and are unwilling that I should run the line immediately. Your presence with troops will produce the most happy results."[19]

So Dade had bid goodby to Pensacola and set sail for one of the most isolated areas to which an American soldier had ever been sent. Down the west coast of Florida for three hundred miles they passed not a single habitation and when they cast anchor in the Bay of Espiritu Santo (Tampa Bay), Pensacola was still the nearest town of any consequence. The colonel had been ordered "to Tampa Bay . . . where he will establish a military post." As to exact location, "he will select a position with a view to health and in reference to the location of the Florida Indians, about to be removed to that vicinity agreeably to the late treaty." Beyond that, it was up to him.[20]

Eleven years had passed since then and a lot of changes had taken place around the bay, but Major Dade, riding confidently at the head of his command some fifty miles north of that early landfall on this second mission to overawe the savages, could well remember.

They had sailed into a bay of noble proportions, running twenty-five miles northeast where it branched in two, the principal portion being the Western, or Tampa, Bay, the

18. The salient terms of the Treaty of Moultrie Creek are given in Boyd, *Florida Aflame*, p. 26.
19. Gadsden to Brooke, December 1, 1823, quoted in Grismer, p. 55.
20. Major General Brown E. Kirby to Brooke, November 5, 1823, quoted in Grismer, p. 55.

smaller Hillsborough Bay, so named for the mouth of the river that discharged into its north shore. On the point of land separating the two there had stood a newly trimmed pole and from its top had fluttered a muslin flag. A note was found attached to the pole from Colonel Gadsden stating that he was camped at the intersection of river and bay awaiting Colonel Brooke.

During a pleasant interim of several days while Gadsden and Brooke explored various sites around the bay, Dade and most of the other officers went ashore on both Egmont and Mullet Keys in the mouth of the bay proper, taking their guns with them for a little hunting and exploring. On the keys, as well as up and down the shore of the bay, there had been no evidence of human habitation—only mangroves along the bay shore, and on the keys, live oak, cedar, and cabbage palm. The only voices besides their own were the lonely sea birds and the crows.[21] The major could remember the bright winter sun and the splendid isolation they had all felt as the first official military settlers in an area that was surely destined to grow as the natives were subdued and settlers from the southern states found it safe to immigrate. From the great stands of timber that could be seen far inland on the rising ground all around the bay and the lush green foliage of the tropical growth that crowded its way in places almost to the water's edge, it was evident that earth and sun and water were lying ready at hand for the control and development of man. Slaves and other workers could soon clear the wild growth and put the land to use in the cultivation of sugar cane and the production of every variety of vegetable. Perhaps busy wharves would someday line the shore and the sails of a dozen nations would billow with the soft tropical breeze of Tampa Bay. When other eyes would one day look across a crowded bay at the works of man, would they remember that Francis Dade and a few companions had first trod these lonely shores?

21. McCall, p. 130.

By the fifteenth, Gadsden and Brooke had determined on the site of the camp. "We are situated on the northeast bank of the Hillsborough River immediately on its entrance into the Bay of the same name. . . . On visiting several places and after a consultation, we determined upon this place as the [most] eligible regarding the objects of the expedition, health and the convenience of getting supplies. We were also influenced by the quantity of cleared land which was at once adapted to gardens for the officers and men." [22] Four miles north of the point where Colonel Gadsden had left his muslin flag, a very pleasing discovery had been made which determined the choice—a good frame house, cleared fields, and a dock. Mr. Robert Hackley, pioneer extraordinary, lived in solitary style, "the only bonafide settler on the entire West Coast." [23] With typical military presumption Colonel Brooke had simply ordered Hackley off his own land and appropriated his holdings— lock, stock, and barrel. It was a command decision, a responsibility Dade, McCall, and other junior officers did not have to share. The decision was made, the site selected, and their job had been to create a military camp.

Within a few weeks the men under Captain Dade had assisted in clearing the land north from the rear of the camp and, in the pine woods, cutting timber for log barracks for officers and men. These rapidly took shape in the expanded clearing, rising twelve feet high under the huge parasol spread of magnificent live oak trees. Even in these early months of the year the temperature was 75 to 80 degrees and the shade provided was welcome. At the suggestion of Colonel Gadsden, the camp was named Cantonment Brooke in honor of the commanding officer who returned the compliment by naming the point of land where the muslin flag was found after the engineer, James Gadsden. The cantonment soon had attained a respectable size with barracks buildings and other structures clustered about. It was no

22. Brooke to Brown, February 5, 1824.
23. Grismer, p. 58.

longer a cantonment but a fort with block houses within the pickets. And Fort Brooke it had remained—a symbol of governmental security in a wild and untamed country.[24]

For almost twenty years now Dade had served up and down the Territory of Florida and the major events of his adult life had taken place here, from Pensacola to Key West. It was in Pensacola, on a Thursday evening, December 6, 1827, that he had been "legally united, according to approved form, in the state of Matrimony" by the Episcopal Rector Charles Hardy.[25] His bride was Amanda Malvina Middleton, sixteen years old[26] and eldest daughter of Isaac Middleton, a carpenter.[27] He and Amanda had made their home in Pensacola in a large, comfortable frame house located less than a mile from the bay on Palafox Street, which they occupied all too rarely. In January, 1831, he had been home on furlough during the birth of their only child, Fannie Langhorne.[28] Now, both Amanda and Fannie waited for him in Key West. It would be good to get home.

During the morning another far-flung cabin had been sighted off to the right, about opposite the intersection of their road with the branch running off northwest to Chocachatti. The intersection continued to the right toward the little knoll a quarter of a mile away where wanderlust had brought another eager settler whose log dwelling stood

24. McCall, p. 133.
25. Copy of marriage license in Dade file, N.A.R.S., also reported in Pensacola *Gazette and West Florida Advertiser,* December 14, 1827.
26. Five different statements as to her age have been brought to light, each made by Amanda Dade, and four of the five giving different years. These are, in order, as follows: 1840 census, Escambia County, Florida (age 29); 1850 census, Escambia County (age 39); application for bounty land in 1853 (age "about 40"); 1860 census, Escambia County (age 45); application for restoration of her name to the pension roll in 1865 (age 49). The author has chosen the year 1811 as her true birth date for several reasons: first, it was twice attested to by Mrs. Dade while each of the other years have only one vote each; second, the female tendency to grow old more slowly as the years progress; and finally, if one were to accept one of the latter years as her birth year, then her age at marriage slips alarmingly from 16 years old to 14, then 12, and finally 11.
27. 1850 census, Escambia County, Florida.
28. Pensacola *Gazette,* September 2, 1848.

isolated and still.[29] Fort Brooke might maintain the integrity of the bay and imply government power over the lonely stretches of rich pine barrens, but when Seminoles were on the move the security of the fort extended only to those within its walls. This was high, rich country abounding in good water and perfect climate and every few miles you could find another cabin perched on a hill where hard, quiet men worked like beasts of burden to provide sustenance for lonely, bonnetted wives to whom soap was a luxury. With the threat of flame and tomahawk upon the land, they'd leave the mouldboard in the furrow, take their sturdy children, and walk the military road until they found safety for their families—then, as likely as not, join with the volunteers for a week, a month, or a year doggedly seeking the restive red men, chase them out or kill them and when they were gone God knows where, draw their pay if they could and return with grateful wives and wondering children to a lonely cabin.

To Francis Dade, officer and gentleman, the isolation of frontier life held no charm, but passing through this less desolate area of the Territory where no less than three trails tramped by white men joined the Fort King Road within two miles and abandoned cabins stared reproachfully across weed grown and stump-filled gardens, it was clear that some men must carry the obligation to provide safety for these illiterate and often ignorant men and women who would follow fading hopes along civilization's ragged edge. These people could plant their own roots along with collard greens, string beans, and corn, while the man with the sword must be content with honor.

The steep hills of yesterday were subdued now and the land flowed gently, working its way toward the Withlacoochee River. The entire visible growth seemed to be the great pillars of long leaf yellow pines, rich smelling in the bright sunlight and with fallen needles carpeting the

29. Original government survey, township 24S, range 21E, section 22, plat and field notes.

earth in autumn brown. The sun was high and clear and Dade could feel the warmth soak through, dispelling the damp and chill of other days. As he moved his horse up and down the column he could see that for the men on foot the sun was perhaps a little more than they might have chosen; sweat was darkening shirts and all coats were packed. The clink of canteens carried to him as thirst was stimulated and assuaged and hot leather caps bobbed off here and there and huge handkerchiefs mopped wet foreheads.

By the middle of the day the command made its closest approach so far to the Withlacoochee River as it wound indirectly north from its source in a vast swamp far to the southeast. From here the river swung east by north, then north, and two miles farther it would turn directly west to cross their path in a channel that had cut its way in ages past through a high pine bluff. From their position at midday the road turned and headed for that point, a path that provided high, firm ground right up to the water rather than the long, sloping approach of floodland.

A short halt for food and rest and the inexorable march continued. The pines that had seemed unending now began to give way to increasing numbers of moss-laden blackjack oaks and the undulating land became almost flat again. Conditions were perfect for the tropical palmetto here beyond the flood line, and the trunks lay in tangled profusion, each with a hundred roots tying it to the earth. Their rich green fronds crowded into the road where passing traffic had kept the trunks from intruding, and the double column of soldiers tramped closer together to avoid the saw-tooth stems and fronds that moved with a dry and hollow rustle in the wind. A breeze from the southeast brought the smell of water to them from the marshland bordering the bend of the river and until they were almost upon it, those in the advance guard who had not traveled the road before did not know that the west-flowing river lay directly ahead. The deep, narrow cut was so banked with palmetto that from eye level the sea of greenery seemed to continue uninterrupted. Then the word was passed and the column slowed while Pacheco was sent ahead, followed by Dade and the advance guard.

The bridge still stood, blackened here and there by fires that had not quite done their job. The main structure looked to be solid enough, only the planking was burnt clean through and a little mending would fix that. Tonight the men would sleep dry.[30]

Quickly now a crew was made up to check the supports while others replaced what few planks were necessary for a careful crossing. The beasts that drew cannon and wagon were led across, picking their way with care. The men followed, grateful for a safe, dry passage. The fifty-foot-wide stream rushed below them, hurrying west and north to the sea, echoing back to them the heavy tread of boots.

The crossing was completed by the time the sun was hidden by tall trees, the men filing down off the bridge and past the smug six-pounder, its blunt black nose pointing disdainfully across the underbrush.

Hurried orders reformed the column and put it in motion, preceded by the small advance guard and bracketed by flankers beating their way noisily through almost impenetrable thickets of scrub oak and dry swamp grass. Long evening shadows were settling here where the woods grew thick and Dade was determined that before night locked them in they should clear the dangerous confinement where maneuvering was impossible. The road north of the river veered to the left and stretched out for high ground not far ahead where they could make camp with a fair chance if the Seminoles should try an attack. Constant urging by the

30. In an article (undated) from the Portland *Daily Advertiser* (quoted in "Personal Reminiscences," p. 71), Ransom Clarke states: "at [the] Big Withlacoochee, where the bridge was partially destroyed . . . by mending it a little we got our wagon and cannon over and got over ourselves." Thus, as Belton was to state, "three out of four bridges are destroyed," but *damaged* would perhaps have been more accurate. In substantiation of Clarke's memory is the diary entry by Lieutenant Duncan on February 18, 1836 (not quite eight weeks after Dade's passage): "come to large Withlacoochee . . . bridge half burned, could have been repaired in one hour. . . ."

noncoms kept the men moving, weary legs pumping yard by yard until, after a mile, they emerged from the worst of the brush and walked again in rising pine land. Rapidly left behind were the danger-filled lowlands of their third river and there was just one more to go.

This close to the river there were too many low spots, ponds, and semi-arid swamps for the temperamental pine to thrive, though many trees struggled in spite of excess water on their roots. Others stood with stunted trunks branching not far above the ground as evidence of a shallow limestone layer an equal distance below ground level, branching roots inevitably causing a corresponding action in the limbs. The result was a grotesque, crippled look in gaunt limbs that twisted strangely against the still bright western sky. Close underbrush had given way to palmetto again, not as thick or tall as that south of the river and hurrying men drew reassurance from the widening view available. Voices that had warned of the danger and spoken in hopeless tones since leaving Fort Brooke were losing faith in their own forebodings while increasing confidence in Major Dade, together with the prospect of camp, warm fires, and food, gave the troopers new heart. Tired and cold, they hurried on.

Through the woods, beyond range of the flankers, dark figures lay watching. The proud men on horseback had passed, then the bobbing heads of soldiers two by two, the trundled gun, and last, the rear guard. When the last figure moved in silhouette past the setting sun, a silent watcher rose slowly here and there to look after them as they dwindled and faded away toward the north. Then, without a word, each turned away into the woods and set out at a steady pace to follow in the night.[31]

Ten miles ahead, deep in the fastness of the Wahoo Swamp and east of the river, Jumper cautioned once again

31. Alligator statement in Sprague, p. 90, "our scouts . . . reported each night their place of encampment."

against a premature move. Warriors who moved in the firelight spoke against letting the white men escape, for this was the second night that attack had been planned and again the soldiers had slipped through the constricting tangle on the banks of the Weewa Thlock Ko and rested now on high and open land. There would be only one more such crossing and after that only Tallaloko the palmetto and Chuli the pine would offer their lesser protection to the men who must fight for the whole Seminole people.

Jumper was adamant. Already Osceola's plans had brought them extra guns and lead and powder from the agent himself. Better that they wait one more day, when Osceola would join them and could lead an attack to certain victory. The white men had still nearly half their way to go—at least four more times would Hasse, the sun, cross over them—and the road ahead offered many chances to a clever man. Perhaps even this night Osceola would return from his work at the agency making possible an early attack tomorrow, but for this night, they would wait and watch in patience; there would be no attack.

In the camp two miles north of the Big Withlacoochee River, Captain Upton Fraser wrote a message by firelight. The miniature breast pin in his shirt front caught the light as he alternately wrote and stared into the flames. He had not had occasion to write more urgently or with more feeling since June 10, 1814, during the last war with England—when he had written a letter of acceptance and appreciation of his first commission as ensign in the Fifteenth Infantry.[32]

Twenty-one years had passed and now he wrote to his friend John Mountfort who was somewhere, presumably, back down the road toward Tampa. He no longer urged speed for it had become quite clear that a junction of the two forces was out of the question; instead he wrote a simple recital of their situation. Each day they had seen sign indicating that the Seminoles had been watching the camp every

32. Fraser file, N.A.R.S.

night and were keeping close watch on their progress, and more than once they had been able to hear them out in the darkness. It had taken no urging to set all hands working on defenses at each bivouac, and they had no choice but to move on each morning. He wrote that the messenger Private Aaron Jewell had returned safely to the command, coming in at eleven o'clock on the night of the twenty-fifth. There was no date on the letter—it seemed unimportant—but he signed it and after putting it in a scrap of oiled paper, placed it unobtrusively in the entrenchment.[33]

There wasn't much sense to it. If they got through he could tell Mountfort whatever he wanted, and if they didn't make it—why then, a little note detailing their danger on the road would have little significance—their bodies would speak more eloquently. But in the evening, when the men were stretched as still as corpses along the ground and the moon, as white as bone, shown dimly through the tall pine tops, it helped a little to put down words that might, sooner or later, be read by a friend. His memory kept dredging up the scene at Fort Brooke the morning they had left when several of the friendly chiefs had crossed the river to bid them a solemn farewell. Quietly, but sadly, they had assured the officers that they were doomed, "That they should never see them again alive."[34] Well, it would be over in a few more days, one way or another. With a last, long look across the sleeping camp and beyond the light to the sentinels who kept watch for them all, he pulled a blanket tight around him and lay down to restless dreams.

33. The only record of the existence of this first, but little known, note written by Fraser occurs in Duncan's diary entry for February 18, 1836: (after crossing the Big Withlacoochee) "march two miles further and encamp[.] [N]ote found from Capt. F(raser) directed to Maj. M[ountfort] found in old entrenchment. . . ." For the substance of the note, we have assumed it to be substantially that of a later note as mentioned in Belton to Jones, January 1, 1836. The "scrap of oiled paper" is an assumption by the author since the note was still legible nearly eight weeks and many rains later.

34. Report in Gardiner file.

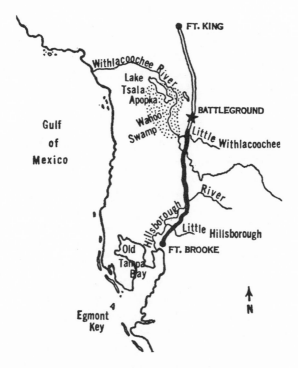

THE FIFTH DAY

Sunday, December 27, 1835

B Y MORNING the wind had shifted back to the northeast and the clean fresh smell of pine sap and needles was pungent on the little knoll where dirty, bearded men stood in small groups around a fire. Increasing wonder at the absence of attack through four days of exposure was tempered by the remarks of veterans who claimed that this day would be the real test. This day they'd run the gauntlet. If anybody thought it was touch and go back there at the Hillsborough or the Withlacoochee, they were in for a surprise. Ransom Clarke there could tell them. The next eight or ten miles was real Seminole country, low and wet, with underbrush that blocked a white man's view to less than ten feet. For an Indian, of course, it was different.

115

They'd be in there, all right. Hadn't they heard them nearly every night and seen signs. But then an Indian could see and smell and sense things like an animal, and like an animal you could pass within a few feet of one and never know he was there unless he chose to tell you with a bullet or a knife. Yes sir, flankers had better be on the job today and any man that wanted to make camp tonight had better keep his eyes open and his musket primed and them that got through with nothing worse than a hungry gut would be the lucky ones.

The dregs of coffee sizzled as they were tossed on smouldering logs and quiet men turned away to check their equipment and assimilate their fear. Along with veterans who could boast of battles fought and danger endured were other men who had volunteered in the heady atmosphere of patriotism and who now felt cut off and isolated from the country and the people they had volunteered to save. Tailors who had put down their shears and tape; teachers who had left the classroom; two shoemakers from New Jersey; a carpenter from Virginia; an Irish hairdresser; printers; lampmakers; and a painter. They had laid aside the tools and the comforts and the safety of their trades and put on uniforms and taken up muskets for the most part because they had pride in their country—native or adopted—and because the food, if not good, was at least regular. Some, like Aaron Jewell, had served barely a year, others for two or three, but soldiering was not a profession with them. They'd serve their time and march where they were told, but they took no delight in danger and had no yearning for death. They stowed their gear and rolled their packs and tried not to think of what the day might hold and turned instead to whatever private thoughts and signs they could conjure as talismans against disaster.

By half-past seven the day's march had begun. The entrenchment was left behind, absurdly inadequate but abandoned with regret. Between the logs a note fluttered like a pale leaf.

After the first mile they left the simple hills that were the single well-drained portion of the six-mile interval between the Big and Little Withlacoochee. A last look back showed dim lines of the earth with curves as gentle as a woman's, the horizon nearly obscured by distant pines and the nearby live oaks and tall winter grass of the savannas. Within a few strides the hills had disappeared completely and the land seemed to close in about them. Head-high grass as thick as bundled wheat made the road a tunnel as it burgeoned from waves of dry marshland that seemed to flow forever toward the swamps ahead. There was little talk as each man's eyes searched the shifting screen beside him. The ranks were closed up tight now, a man stumbling here and there as he trod on the hurrying boot heels of the man ahead. Then suddenly, without a noticeable rise, they were out of the grass and moving across a low shoulder that stood like an island in spite of its insignificant elevation. Every spring rain would submerge the savannas but knolls like this frequently passed season after season above water and the change of vegetation was as abrupt as fear. The ground cover here was low and green and tall pines clustered like royalty, their feet out of water and arms spread in blessing high above the common oaks whose twisted shapes seemed to kneel about the edges of the mounds, clothed in rags of tattered moss. The advancing men slowed their steps for a moment's reassurance as they passed these islands in a dry sea. Compared to the prairies the view was good, revealing on all sides more of the same—winter grass set about here and there with a hickory or an oak, perhaps a clump of palmetto brilliant green in the sunlight. A few more strides and they could see only the grass by their sides and the backs of their companions. There was a certain reassurance in the fact that the length of the column was great enough that some portion of it was nearly always crossing a slight elevation and these moments were fully occupied in scanning the waves in the sea of grass for any movement that might give warning of the presence of Indians. The advance, the rear, and flank guards loosely wrapped the command in a thin line of warning but the men knew that if the stealthy Seminole wished to strike he could belly up along the line of march, easily missed by the guard, and be lying in wait just here, or there—a small dark patch like a scrap of moss, never seen until it rose in a blur of motion while fear curdled a cry and a sharp knife could stab and stab again. The men marched close and there were no stragglers.

For an hour and a half the road led gradually northwest, then gradually due north past a pond more distinct than most, several feet deep in grass grown water, the dark blue of the surface twinkling through the green reeds, an abode of giant frogs who fed silent, implacable snakes of a half-dozen varieties that were food in turn for alligators that moved in season from pond to pond. Sunning themselves here and there were hard- and soft-shelled turtles, viewing the sunlight through cold, reptilian eyes and listening to the incomprehensible sound of an army's booted feet. Swinging gently around the pond, the road continued north, then slightly east to avoid another good-sized and water-filled lake, threading its way from knoll to knoll, carefully missing the greater depressions and the summit of the mounds, for level travel was faster travel. There was no real safety here and speed was the only substitute. If and when the high ground beyond the little river was reached a reasonable chance might be expected, but the only chance offered here was in swift departure.

Two more miles they continued northeast while the knolls grew smaller and the ponds became less frequent. The land was more nearly level and the only open view was the path ahead. The saw grass gave way to impenetrable thickets of oak and hickory where eighty men had labored to hack out the road with felling axes in 1826.[1] It had been hard and heavy work, but then the Seminole had not been aroused to a killing pitch and the only danger was disease. Now no clearing was required other than a little cutting by the advance as they passed first through the

1. McCall, p. 193.

infringing arms of the border trees though the men who followed were sweating like the axemen of 1826. Not far ahead was the Little Withlacoochee, and those who had passed this way before were sure that there at the crossing was the place for a Seminole attack.

Ransom Clarke knew the spot. They were swinging in a shallow arc to the northwest and this drier ground with the worn shoulders of rock beneath his boots was easy to remember. The river was one more mile and they'd be lucky if they didn't have to wade half the distance. From here on the land was so low in its approach to the small channel of the affluent that even in the dry winter season .it sometimes remained in the condition of marshland. The haunt of crawling things and stunted oaks where palmetto and saw grass struggled together like crippled cousins—one too wet and the other too dry. But at least he could see, for there was little growth that stood more than waist high and far ahead the jagged tops of cypress and live oak sawed at the sky. That was the bank of the creek-sized river where thirsty roots could sink deep into sodden ground and raise tall trunks. He knew the long high approach that had been thrown up when the road was new, beginning several hundred feet this side of the river and rising gradually through the scrub and oak thickets until it was at least ten feet above the water when it reached the bank.[2] The old bridge was surely burnt and that meant they'd struggle through the thickets to reach the shore and then, when they were spread out across the narrow stream with some men in the water while the rest were split in half, one group on the north shore and the other on the south, both half-hidden in underbrush, that would be the time for attack. It seemed impossible that men with better sense were here —the major up there on his horse, and Gardiner, Fraser, and the rest with a hundred troopers marching along behind

2. When the retracing of the Fort King Road was done in December, 1963, this crossing was missed in the tremendously heavy growth. However, in November, 1964, William Goza and the author revisited the area and were able to find the old approaches, matching exactly the route designated on the old survey.

like sheep to slaughter—when no man among them did not
know by now what they were facing. In an hour they could
be under the guns and knives of the Seminole Nation
without the slightest chance to pull through, yet all around
him men continued to march on and it didn't make any
sense at all.

This was the crisis. As well as any man and better than
most, Major Dade knew the danger. Riding behind the
advance guard and well ahead of the main column, he sent
again for the Negro Pacheco. Better that one man risk
drawing enemy fire than the whole command. Silent and
frightened, the slave rode slowly forward the last few
hundred yards where the road ran straight, then up the
slope that carried the road to the edge of the river. Here,
sunlight full upon him and in view of the major who
waited with the guard, he scanned the country quickly for
any immediate sign of ambush. Panicky moments slipped
by while nothing moved except cheerful birds high in the
trees which stood in serried ranks and solemn guard along
the low banks.

The crossing had been constructed across a loop in the
river and the stream, flowing from the right around a curve
toward the crossing piled in ridges against the trestles standing in dark shallow water, then spilled off and joined the
smoothly flowing stream that passed by and gathered to
the left in a large pool against the base of the high sand bluff
whose matted growth of palmettos held firm against the
never-ending wash. North, beyond the slowly circling pool,
the river flowed on, disappearing again to the left between
rising banks of white sand. Ahead, beyond the burned
remnants of the bridge that hung like a torn net above the
water, Pacheco could see only the ten-foot bluff of the other
half of the ramp and past it the tunnel-like opening of the
road as it eased back down through the undergrowth and
vines. Anything might be lurking there but nothing that
moved. Nothing that would give the major any more reason
to turn back than what they had already passed.

Dade watched as the Negro wheeled about and headed back. Without a word said he had received the principal information that he wanted in the fact that the interpreter was still alive. If Osceola and his warriors planned a surprise attack he'd have to count on the flankers flushing them, but if even one man could be safely exposed then it was quite possible that this river, like the last two, could be crossed without incident. As an officer of the United States Army he was not paid to seek security and there was no point at all in dwelling on the ever-present possibilities of entrapment or ambush. There was really only one hope for himself and his command and he knew it: that the threat of vast armed might would overawe the disorganized, barbaric people of Florida and stay them from any rash move against his one-hundred. Any fear shown to his men or to the eyes he felt were always upon them might precipitate trouble and would gain them nothing. If the crossing was to be challenged it might just as well come now.

The guards far out on the right and left flanks of the road maintained their perilous positions while orders were given for the advance to make their crossing, fan out on the north shore, and prepare to cover the crossing of the main body. The moment of indecision was past and it was better to do anything than to do nothing. Up and down the long blue column fear was tempered with relief as the men heard the commands and knew that they were off the dead center point of inaction.

By the time the advance guard had waded through the waist-deep water, icy cold but no more than twenty feet wide, the rythmic sound of chopping thudded solidly in the air. A good-sized pine was brought down, smashing the lesser growth as it stabbed the ground with a dozen broken limbs. Before it had fairly settled men attacked it again, trimming off the stumps of limbs on the underside and cutting with single, clean swipes those that still rose tall and needled from the fallen trunk. Ready hands grasped it from butt to tip and a double line of men carried it to the river.

A pair of men at the edge of the water and others behind them passed it forward hand over hand until the long, slender top reached to and then beyond the far bank. On signal it was dropped and a few men crossed carefully, scuffing their boots across the crisp bark, brushing it off like flakes of rust, their arms extended for balance while they stared fixedly at the narrowing bridge before their feet. Once over, they took up the long, limbless trunk and carried it up the shallow bank until the log lay level from bank to bank several feet above the water. Thus far there had been no sign or sound of Seminoles and confidence was growing.

The mounted officers of the first company led out into the water while the men began crossing on the log bridge,[3] hurried on by men behind them who were bunching up as their double column blended into a single line at the river bank. On each shore men were spread out in a semicircle through the brush, muskets at the ready and watching with painful attention for any sign of trouble. Like sand through an hourglass, the group on the south shore slowly dwindled through a single thin line that spanned the dark rush of water, while the contingent on the north shore gradually increased and reformed into a double file that moved up the road to make room for those who followed. Through the shallow water the teams on both the wagon and the six-pounder dragged their burdens through. More and more quickly the remainder of the men hurried over, for no man wanted the distinction of being alone even for a moment at a place like this. And before the rear guard was well across, the command was given to move out and from the oldest veteran to the newest recruit they pushed along eagerly, relieved and incredulous at their peaceful passing through an unsprung trap.

3. This mode of crossing is based again on Duncan, who wrote on February 19, 1836, that upon reaching the Little Withlacoochee "all cross on log . . . horses ford. . . ." Thus it seems that a log crossing was acceptable to the military, would certainly have been more practical than fording, and seems the obvious course for Dade's command.

Minutes later the order to halt fell on impatient ears. Word passed back that fresh Indian sign had been found— the prints of three separate men clear in the trail. Shortly the column jostled into motion; the judgment being that the prints belonged to friendly runners who had been sent out a few days previously from Brooke to King.[4]

Three-quarters of a mile up the road, on higher ground and by the shore of a lake that flooded several acres, the advance passed an Indian village.[5] On the flank, guards moved up cautiously, muskets primed and bayonets fixed. It looked deserted, but you could never tell about Indians. Silently, watchfully, the column in the military road moved by while singly and in pairs the men on the flank investigated the empty dwellings and poked among the discarded household items that lay about. The number of structures indicated a sizable gathering of Seminoles, but the entire area, hard-packed by the passing of many moccasined feet, was silent. A few wildflowers turned delicate faces to the sun and the musky warm smell of dry palmetto fronds that thatched the buildings filled the air with the strong, peaceful smell of human habitation. There was no danger and nothing of value; the guard moved on.

It was past midday before the river had been left well behind and the shortest possible stop made for eating. Confidence gave more strength than the meager rations, and the major, encouraged now and more determined than ever to make good on their gamble, rushed them through and back on the road. Somewhere between the two rivers they had passed the halfway point and now he had only one goal—Fort King. If the Seminoles let them pass unmolested for just a few more miles they should be relatively safe, for back at the little river they had actually passed through the southern tip of the ominous Wahoo Swamp, stronghold of the Seminole Nation. Within its trackless depths stretch-

4. Ransom Clarke in the Portland *Daily Advertiser,* quoted in "Personal Reminiscences," p. 72.
5. Duncan diary, entry for February 19, 1836.

ing northwest for forty miles along the Withlacoochee, any
number of Indians could live off the land for a lifetime and
remain nearly impervious to the attacks of white men.
From it they could strike a thousand separate blows and
retreat without a trace, camping first on one dry knoll and
then another, their passage lost in the endless shallow water-
ways that kept thousands of acres permanently submerged.
But the Fort King Road, leading north and west to higher
ground, was putting more distance between the command
and the swamp with every step and already the flora was
changing in reaction to the elevation. The impassable
thickets of scrub oak and underbrush interspersed with dry
ponds of tall saw grass had given way to stands of second
rate pine and low palmetto. Again the hills were rising a
few feet above the general level and the still dry ponds were
sinking lower. The contrast was a welcome change, though
these scrubby pine barrens were by no means a forest. By
noon tomorrow they would be in the first of many pine
forests where the underbrush, even palmetto, was smothered
in the fall of needles and there would be little cover for an
attacking force. The enemy who had ignored their passage
through sixty miles of swamp and tangled brush would not
risk battle with trained and disciplined troops during the
remaining forty miles of dry and open woodlands. The sun
was perched on the tree tops left of the road and the gauntlet
was nearly run.

In the dense cover above Fort King, Osceola, patient as
death, still lay in wait. Only yards away a wagon stood
outside the door of the sutler's combined home and store.
Inside, the sutler was working with his two assistants, boxing
up his goods for storage inside the fort. Farther on, in the
shadow of the wall surrounding the fort, General Thompson
worked in his office. During the day Osceola had seen that
the gates in the wall were generally left open, with most
of the single remaining company working outside the pickets
securing and strengthening the defenses, obviously expect-

ing that an attack, if it came, would strike from the north and east where the hammock fronted and flanked the fort.[6] The chief and his followers lay unmoving and unseen through the long chilly hours of the day, concealed by the thick palmetto hammock from which attack was anticipated. But Osceola did not plan to storm the fort. Though he had come with that intention, several days of watchful waiting had assured him that it would not be necessary.[7] With the departure of three companies, there were hardly more men left in the fort than he himself commanded, and the advantage of surprise would be with the attackers. But he had no real interest in the palisaded structure, or the men in it, for that matter. He was interested in just one white man and that one spent most of the daylight hours outside the walls. He would wait, and when the right moment came he would take it.

But other Seminoles were not so patient. Within the depths of the Wahoo Swamp, east of the river and almost directly west of the position where more than a hundred men marched in double file, Jumper, Alligator, and Micanopy sat in council. No longer did Jumper urge delay, for the old chief Micanopy had finally arrived. No longer was patience a virtue. It was clear that Osceola had not yet accomplished his mission at the fort and Jumper knew him well enough to be sure that he would not join them until then. But the soldiers were traveling steadily and soon the last favorable moment would pass.[8]

Micanopy was cautious—Alligator thought him even timid—as he sat stolid and dull-eyed, listening in silence and then urging delay. He wanted no part in the white man's plan for the removal of the Seminoles to the western lands, but even less he wanted war. Perhaps, given enough time, the white man would change his views—would relent and

6. Harris to Gibson, December 30, 1835, given in Boyd, *Florida Aflame*, p. 71.
7. Sprague, p. 89.
8. Statement by Alligator in Sprague, p. 90.

let them live in peace—but if they should take up arms in
outright attack as Osceola and Jumper proposed there would
be no chance for them—the white men would bring more
and more of the soldiers and life would be an endless
struggle. Peace—that was the important thing.

Against the words of appeasement Jumper marshaled
the deeds of the white men—the deceit and death they had
brought, the indignity and suffering—his peculiar voice
holding his listeners in thrall. The camp, lit by pine torches,
was crowded with one hundred and eighty warriors and
beyond the shifting perimeter of light lay dark and brooding
swamp. The voice of Jumper rose and fell, carrying his
listeners with him, and when he turned at last to Micanopy,
the old chief could only accede to the overwhelming demands of the entire group. Osceola or not, they would leave
at dawn.[9]

A few miles to the east, Seminole scouts kept patient
watch over the soldiers who had come in daylight to a clear,
deep pond and halted for the night.[10] Watching from the
cover of darkness and dense palmetto, the scouts could see
the officers seated apart, eating and talking while the soldiers
moved about in the glare of their tremendous fire.

To the tired soldiers around the fire the guards were only
silhouettes beyond the leaping flames, their cloaked forms
outside the barricade shifting like shadows in the night. The
temperature was dropping steadily and the minds of the
sentries were more on weariness and cold than on Seminoles.
Even the major seemed to think that there was little danger
now and he ought to know. Here and there around the fire
a few men noticed the changes in attitudes that had grown
more and more tangible during the final hours of the day.
Some men seemed unnaturally cheerful, almost as though
they had crossed the Jordan rather than the Little Withla-

9. *Ibid.*, p. 90.
10. Ransom Clarke in the Portland *Daily Advertiser,* quoted in "Personal
Reminiscences," p. 71. Lieutenant Duncan states on February 19, 1836: "march
on to the last camp of . . . Maj. Dade . . . find pond of good water."

coochee and thereafter had been climbing the golden stairs with every step, their voices as gay and bantering as school-boys with an unexpected holiday. But there were others who didn't seem to share the optimism. To an old timer like Sergeant John Vailing,[11] a veteran of nine years in the artillery and now almost forty years old, it would take more than high hopes to erase the threat of possibly a thousand hostiles when they still had forty miles to go. Years ago he had served in the expedition against Black Hawk, and since then he had had dealings with a good many other Indians. The experiences had not given him much confidence in threats and gestures—numbers were the thing that counted. They were still in mortal danger and he knew that at least Captain Fraser shared his concern. He could see the captain sitting apart from the other officers, writing again as he had done the night before[12] and he wondered what possible use the messages could have. For seven years he'd served with the captain, but never in a tight spot like this. Perhaps the messages were just his way of worrying. Around the fire there were other worriers too, but maybe the rest of the men were better off in their feeling of security. Neither attitude would change the outcome if Osceola was waiting for them and at least those with confidence would get a good night's sleep.

11. Enlistment records and personal file on Sergeant Vailing, N.A.R.S.
12. Reference is made to this second message in Belton to Jones, January 1, 1836: "a note from Capt. Frazer [*sic*] . . . which was fastened in a cleft stick and stuck in a creek dated . . . on the 27th." Since only *one* note has heretofore been mentioned in connection with the command, it should be pointed out that this later note was brought into Fort Brooke on January 1, while the earlier note, as we have seen, was found on February 18.

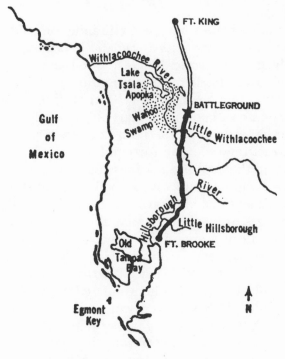

THE LAST DAY

Monday, December 28, 1835

ALONG the high west rim of a pale green pond an army slept. One hundred men lay wrapped in blankets beneath great oaks while orange flames lanced the night and sentries waited for the dawn. The chill of yesterday had dropped to bitter cold during the night and soldiers turned in uneasy sleep. The guards, shoulders hunched against the wind blowing down the trail from the northeast, turned alternately from the fire to stare out into the blackness beneath the trees. No sound broke the silent cold outside the low log wall.

Near the fire Major Francis Langhorne Dade awoke in darkness. Staring up through the hovering limbs of giant oaks, he felt a wave of exultation wash through him like a draft of brandy. They had come more than half the distance to Fort King and the valley of the shadow lay behind them. Five days of slow traveling through swamp and thick brush cut by four rivers had been a long tough pull, but from here on in it was white man's country—high and wooded—where wet feet could dry and men could maneuver. The Seminoles had lost their last good chance when they let him cross the Little Withlacoochee. Now they were beyond the flood land where Indians could kill and disappear and white men could only die. He had made the boast that with one hundred men he could march through the Indian Nation with impunity[1] and it was beginning to look like a sure thing. With Fort King reinforced, the Indian threat would subside and he could return to Key West and Amanda, perhaps even in time for little Fannie's fifth birthday just a few weeks away.

By seven o'clock the sky was the color of a dirty sheet and the overcast oozed rain that fell like cold sweat. The Fort King Road bordered the north and east sides of the pool— the "round clay sink" Mudge had called it[2]—lying deep within its white clay bank. The temperature was forty-four degrees and blue clad men shivered as they stood in double file. Ransom Clarke waited in the right file, his belly stoked with cold meat, hard bread, and strong coffee. Over the leather caps of the men in front he could see Major Dade. Clarke straightened instinctively—belly in, chest out—for Dade had that effect on a man. The major's legs hugged his horse's ribs below the polished saddle and he held the black leather reins in one white-gloved hand while he waited through the roll call.

The men stood their places, sleepy and uncomfortable, arms folded around their muskets and their hands drawn up in their sleeves to keep warm. The major rode in front of the ranks and faced them. Against the steady drip of rain most of them had already fastened the buttons of their

1. Cohen, p. 231.
2. "Personal Reminiscences," p. 71.

greatcoats over the cartridge boxes on their belts when he
spoke: "I can't tell you to place your guns on the cart . . .
but since it's raining, you may hold them under your
coats."[3] Dry powder wasn't much use in a wet chamber
and it was typical of Dade that with confidence went caution.
It might be awkward to bring guns and powder out from
under their coats if they were attacked, but not as difficult
as if they were under the tarpaulin on the wagon. If skir-
mishers were sighted, they'd get them out fast enough.

By seven o'clock the advance guard had moved out, led
by Lieutenant Robert Rich Mudge. At twenty-five a man
of "conspicuous military ardor" from Lynn, Massachusetts.
He moved proudly, as befitted a West Pointer, and even this
early in the morning he managed to give a certain swagger
to his appearance, from the crossed cannons on his cap to
the crimson sash around his waist. He allowed himself the
small vanity of a chased gold ring on one finger, covered
now by travel-stained white gloves, and in his vest pocket
four gold pieces jingled softly.[4]

In spite of rain, the high ground here was only surface
wet and behind Mudge the men of the advance guard set
the pace with firm steps, in single file. Behind them rode
the major, cheerful and confident. Beside him, uneasy and
withdrawn, rode Captain Fraser.

Louis Pacheco moved with the advance. Bundled in his
coat against the chill wind, the Negro was uneasy. He had
been hired as an interpreter, but they had neither talked
with Indians nor seen any. He had reported Indian sign
to the major many times since they left Fort Brooke, but

3. "Pasco County Thirty Years Ago," Dade City, Fla., *Banner* (date unknown),
presumably quoting Ransom Clarke, though it says merely "an account of a
survivor."
4. The primary source of information on Lieutenant Mudge is the Mudge
file, N.A.R.S. The ring, gold pieces, and so forth are mentioned by various men
of General Gaines' army, Duncan, McCall, and others, who reached the scene
of battle on February 20, 1836. As to the location of Mudge in the column, and
of other officers and men subsequently mentioned, we have relied primarily on
the accounts by Clarke combined with deductions based upon logic and the
evidence as found by General Gaines.

now, unaccountably to him, there were no flankers out. But the major was a Virginian, a southern aristocrat; he didn't welcome advice from black men.

An interval of several hundred yards separated Dade and Fraser from the main column where Captain Gardiner, as short and tough as the little six-pounder, rode at the head of his company. Under the leather cap his hair was partly gray and it was this kind of service that made it so. In the early morning gloom of tall grass, palmetto, and forest it was hard to share Dade's confidence. *Anyplace* was Indian country if an Indian chose to make it so. If Osceola had his braves under half the control of which he boasted, they could look for trouble right up to the end.

He swung around, looking back over the double file in blue that followed, and wondered if the faces glancing up at him could read the uneasiness in his eyes. Good men and true, but God Almighty, what could they do if Osceola called their bluff?

Lieutenant Basinger marched with the rear guard, shoulders squared beneath the golden epaulettes, an aura about him that infected the hardest of the veterans who trudged behind him. In this handsome young soldier each of the tired troopers could see the glamor and glory of war they had once heard about, and for a moment could rekindle memories of enlistment officers and their talk of noble danger shared with brave companions.

Then a gust of cold rain would brush the face of a man like Private Michael Kenny and suddenly the sound of distant trumpets faded and the memory of his wife Ellen doing wash for the men back at the fort brought him back to the cold, danger, and reality of war.[5] Instead of triumphant battles in the sunshine it usually came down to this— a cold and thankless march down a muddy road.

For Private Joseph Wilson danger was a new and fearful thing. He was a musician from Sackett's Harbor, New York, where few dangers were more serious than a sour note.

5. File on Michael Kenny, N.A.R.S.

In response to a call for volunteers to protect the settlers being killed by savages in this new land he'd volunteered for military duty and found himself at thirty-six in the role of soldier—his only instrument a gun. But there were just ten months to go before his enlistment would be up and by next Christmas he'd be home.

And Aaron Jewell, marching with Company C, wondered if he had done the right thing in volunteering. Back at the Big Hillsborough it had looked like a smart move offering to take the major's message to Fort Brooke. Maybe he'd been a damn fool to push his luck and carry the return message to the command. Major Dade and Captain Gardiner might catch a little glory for their volunteering but who'd ever know that he, a private soldier, had risked his neck to ride the trail alone and at night with the woods full of hostiles? Maybe farming back in Vermont hadn't been so bad after all.

Detached portions of companies B, C, and H of the Second Artillery, in route step with six feet between the columns trudged along the beaten path of the Fort King Road, pale blue trousers scissoring endlessly against the tall wet grass along the way. Stiff muscles loosened as the men tramped over sand, lumped and rutted by hooves and boots, the lines weaving as those in the van turned out past rocks that thrust heavy shoulders from the earth or the droppings of the horses, steaming in the cold, gray air. Their damp, heavy greatcoats bulged over their muskets and there was little talk beyond a muttered complaint or jest. Through the misty woods the only sounds were the jingle of harness and the screech of ungreased axles and a steady low pounding of tired feet on wet sand.

At Tampa Bay all hope of a junction between Major Mountfort and the command of Major Dade was gone, even the most optimistic conceding that the five-day interval was too great—and now Greyson was finally sighted. It was early morning when word was brought to Captain Belton that the ship had gotten into the wrong bay, the western branch, and grounded in shallow water. Belton immediately sent out an armed party with a flag as a signal and with instructions for Greyson to land his men right where he was, four miles west of the fort on the east side of Tampa Bay, and march overland to Hillsborough Bay and Fort Brooke. They could never reach Dade and his men but at least they could help man the defenses and protect the wives and children of the command if the anticipated attack on the fort materialized. The Seminole who had been sent out with messages for Thompson and Clinch was two days overdue and the delay was ominous, for it was now nearly four weeks since there had been any contact with the Florida headquarters at Fort King. There was no longer anything they could do for Major Dade, but there were men, women, and children here who must be protected until reinforcements arrived by boat. With the addition of Greyson and his men they should be relatively secure.[6]

North by the Fort King Road, two miles beyond the night's bivouac, the way led east of north, always taking the highest ground through a land that varied no more than ten feet in elevation from pond to knoll. Winter had been mild and dry and the shallow savannas were tall with winter grass.

By eight o'clock the drip of rain had ended. The sky brightened as the sun probed with weak fingers through the thick upper terraces of the wood. Spirits lifted with the sun as every mile brought them farther from the low land of danger and closer to Fort King.

Dr. Gatlin let his mount drift back and forth the length of the column. From the side of the road he watched the men pass until the rear guard bringing the six-pounder had come up. The four horses were leaning hard into the harness, each left-hand mount ridden by a driver with the long shaft of the limber swinging below his right boot and

6. Belton to Jones, January 1, 1836.

the thousand-pound burden of carriage and cannon jolting and swaying awkwardly behind. With a slap of the reins, the doctor moved back up the column, pausing to speak to the other officers as he passed.

Lieutenant John Low Keais, marching with Company B of the Third Artillery Regiment, was an orphan "dependent on his own exertions for his advancement" and was of such moral and intellectual worth that those who knew him best praised him in strong terms that seemed extravagant only to strangers. At home Dr. Gatlin would probably never have been aware of Keais' existence, though they had lived only thirty miles apart, for his own family were people of means. In the enforced circumstances of travel he had discovered the younger man to be knowledgeable on many subjects and particularly adept at mathematics, having mastered the six books of Euclid before entering West Point in 1831, when he was nineteen. He and Lieutenant Henderson had graduated together back in July and were already at Fort Brooke when Gatlin had arrived at the end of November. The three young southern officers had much in common and the exigencies of service drew them together.[7]

Captain Gardiner studied his map. They must be about four miles from last night's camp. He glanced toward the sun directly to his right above the pine tops, dull gold in the fresh-washed sky. Nearly nine o'clock and the column was traveling almost due north. Up ahead Lieutenant Mudge and the advance guard should be about opposite the big pond shown on the map where the road kept to the pine wood just above the high water line. About the time the rear guard left the savanna to enter the woods, Mudge should be past the pond and swinging back to the northeast, the direction they'd hold nearly all the way in to Fort King. Gardiner put away the map and resettled himself in the saddle. They were making good time and with no more rivers to cross they might make it by tomorrow night. Per-

7. Keais file, N.A.R.S.

haps Dade *was* justified in his optimism. The high land and bright sky were certainly a more cheerful prospect than the swamp and the rain.

A patch of light in the brush made him turn sharply and his fingers tightened in the leather reins, but it was just a pale gray horse standing alone, browsing on tall grass between the close growing pines. Pacheco had dropped back from the advance guard to investigate, and Fraser pulled out just ahead of the main body and joined him. As Gardiner passed he could see that the beast was old and bony. The black man was evidently trying to find Indian sign. Gardiner could see no significance in the stray beast and passed on.[8]

From front to rear the detachment stretched in a shallow arc a quarter of a mile long, the large pond the hub around which the line turned. Peaceful, silent country. Too silent. Was it imagination, or were the woods utterly quiet? The sound of their passing seemed suddenly loud in a world that was holding its breath.

Gardiner turned at the sound of Dade's horse as he trotted back up from the rear of the column speaking in a good natured voice to the men. His words were audible: "Have a good heart; our difficulties and dangers are over now, and as soon as we arrive at Fort King you'll have three days rest, and keep Christmas gaily."[9] With a confident smile the major passed, riding forward to follow in the wake of the advance guard. Behind him came Fraser and Pacheco. Captain Gardiner might have brought to the attention of Dade the unnatural silence of the place, but in the face of such enthusiasm the moment passed. And then a single rifle shot burst the silence.

Through the long moment that followed there was no change, no further sound. As though determined to ignore

8. Statement by Pacheco in McKay, II, 480.

9. Clarke account in the Charleston, S.C., *Courier*, August, 1836, quoted in Edward C. Boynton, *History of West Point* (New York, Van Nostrand, 1863), p. 291; with slight changes, the same quote is given in several other sources, but doubtless they too are paraphrasing Clarke's account.

the obscene interruption, the column moved on one more pace. Those in the front ranks of the double file who looked to the major gaped in horror. Francis Dade, broad shoulders erect, slumped gently in his saddle like a bag of grain cut in the middle. His elbows, projecting just past his hips as he held the reins, slid forward to his lap and his black beard touched the mane of his horse as though in a last brush of affection. His body fell to the side, one black boot dragging across the saddle, silver spur gleaming, and then he was gone —a bullet in his heart and dead before he touched the ground.[10]

In the same long moment, twenty yards to the left of the road and paralleling the command from front to rear, painted devils rose up, sprung suddenly like death plants from palmetto and grass. Some knelt, some stood full length; each pine, silent and aloof, concealed its Seminole. Like the ragged crashing of the gates of hell, one hundred and eighty Indian weapons[11] blasted the soldiers at point-blank range, half-inch lead balls bursting through damp wool greatcoats and yielding flesh and shattered bone. With equal suddenness red men and white dropped where they stood, but no Seminole was injured and nearly fifty white men were dead. Wounded troopers jerked and writhed in the trail between the boots of their comrades, staring fearfully at the red flow from punctured wool over arm, hip, and thigh. And then they screamed.

Such had been the shock of the attack that no trigger had yet been squeezed in defense. Unwounded men, Clarke, Wilson, and the rest, stood isolated in the harvested ranks, the cries of comrades at their feet breaking the paralysis of surprise and putting them in motion. Those few who carried loaded and unlimbered weapons fired them for the most part straight in the air in nervous reaction[12] while others, with muskets and ammunition pouches under their

10. McCall, p. 304.
11. Sprague, p. 180.
12. Statement by Clarke in Captain James Barr, *A Correct and Authentic Narrative of the Indian War in Florida* (New York, J. Narine, 1836), p. 9.

coats, fumbled with desperate sobs at the heavy gold and silver buttons.

For Gardiner, the road ahead was suddenly clear. Dade, Fraser, and Mudge were all down and the advance guard with them. He could see the slave Pacheco lying motionless with the guard who were sprawled in single file as they had marched. Their cries were dreadful. The first coherent sound was Gardiner's shout to unlimber the gun as he wheeled toward the men of the main body. And only twenty years of discipline checked his reaction to the change in men who, only seconds before, had been following in trustful confidence with long strides. Strong young bodies lay stretched against the grass, agony-twisted fingers clutching at the sand and blood flowing like tears from a hundred wounds. Those who still stood here and there, dazed and bewildered, fumbled out their weapons while Gardiner impelled them by desperate command into coherent action. By now the enemy had reloaded and once more rose to reap a second but lesser crop. The targets were moving, and haste and poor aim sent the second barrage through the broken ranks to smack the pines along the east of the road like sleet. Only a few men went down, for the captain's commands had broken the spell of fear and sent men to the shelter of the nearest trees. With desperate precision they loaded their muskets, pulling the two-inch paper cartridges from the leather boxes or hand-made pouches on their belts, biting off the twist of paper at the end with clenched and yellow teeth, pouring the first pinch of black powder in the pan and the rest down the smooth barrel that was thick as a man's thumb. The one-ounce ball followed, still in the paper cover, and powder, ball, and paper rammed home with the flared end of the rod; then, with the heavy hammer cocked to strike the frizzle and with bearded cheek against a walnut stock, they searched the swaying grass for the enemy.[13]

13. Interview with gun collector Fred T. Bromley by the author in Dade City, Florida, 1964; also much information on the muskets of the time was given by Milton D. Jones of St. Petersburg, an expert on the weapon.

The few moments' respite between volleys had given stunned minds time to catch up and the unrelenting commands of Gardiner and Basinger, miraculously unhurt, lashed the artillerymen into defensive action. At the first volley the drivers had flogged the double team through the broken files bringing the cannon half-way up the column before the second volley cut the beasts down in their traces and the drivers with them. William Basinger took command as the crew disengaged the carriage trail from the limber. Putting his shoulder to the wooden spokes he helped wheel the cannon around in a quarter-turn to face the attack, then slashed at the harness straps with his sabre to free the gun from the tangle where team and drivers alike sprawled across the trail, the horses great hooves still twitching as muscles slowly died. A six-pound iron ball with powder and wadding was taken from the carriage box, offset near the limber, and the commands, foreshortened, were given in rapid order: "Sponge! Ram! Point!" No time now for sighting—the barrel was pointed toward the west, the elevation screw set for level firing—"Fire!" The *blam* of the cannon encouraged the defenders, and the wounded struggled to rise.[14]

With Basinger in charge of the gun, Gardiner took command of the remainder of the force. Few orders were needed, for those still alive had found refuge behind the thick-boled pines along the east of the trail or lay where they had fallen after the first volley, shoving dead troopers across the line of fire as human breastworks. Dr. Gatlin, unwounded, had taken up a weapon and lay with the men, firing as fast as he could reload. Half his troopers dead, five out of eight officers wounded or dead, facing what appeared to be a thousand Seminoles, Gardiner's last reserve of caution was gone. He stood upright in the trail, his citizen's coat incongruous in the midst of battle, his short tough

14. Based on the chapter "The Practice of Gunnery" in Albert Manucy, *Artillery Through the Ages* (Washington, Government Printing Office, 1949), pp. 79-85.

figure a battery of fury, and his voice a cannon roar of rage: "God *Damn,* God *Damn.*"[15] All down the line his curse was as explicit as a command, his silver sword a baton of courage. Volley after volley from Seminole and soldier blasted the air, but no shot struck him.

The six-pounder, normally served by a crew of eight, was fired by whatever artillerymen Basinger could bring to the piece. The great guns that fired balls the size of grapefruit were a terror to the Indians, yet under the tight command of Jumper and Alligator and emboldened by success they held their ground, watching through the grass for the moment the match was applied, then dropping flat or stepping behind a tree. Steadily they picked off the men around the gun, waiting until the thick smoke drifted away, firing, then dodging back. Rarely, cannister shot would seek them out and the whoop of the battle cry would be varied by a scream of pain. In spite of the casualties—one soldier for nearly every ball fired—the gun continued to send shot and shell across the grass. Now it was not so easy to find the soldiers with the muskets for the dead seemed everywhere in the white man's road, and in the one exposed moment above the grass, a man could fire and drop without knowing if his target were alive or dead.

Gradually the firing was slowing on both sides. The soldiers, outnumbered six to one, thought the odds were even greater.[16] In any case they could do no more than they were doing—either to rush or retreat would mean instant annihilation—so they lay in the damp sand, hot with fear in the chilly morning and firing at every rustle from the palmetto only yards away.

Ote Emathla, or Jumper, lay in a palmetto clump west of the road. This was not the way of Indian fighting and however successful he knew that his warriors would soon want to make a move. He did not have the power over them that

15. Statement by Alligator in Sprague, p. 91.
16. Statements by Thomas, Clarke, and Joseph Sprague in Potter, p. 107.

Osceola had and certainly old Micanopy lying nearby did not, but if he was to continue in charge and keep this seeming victory, he must give them some new word. The young lieutenant and his men still served the fearful black gun, that kept his warriors from rising in a body for a rush, and the brave officer with the sword still swore at his men and kept them firing. There were less than a dozen soldiers unwounded, he was sure, and rather than risk defeat they would do better to leave it at this and withdraw. Later he could confer with Micanopy and Alligator and there would still be time to finish the fight if they should insist.

He looked to each side in turn and with a sweep of his arm gave the signal to withdraw. The signal was passed from man to man and slowly, silently, the Seminoles crawled back through the grass and palmetto. All firing ceased. The first attack was over.

Again the voices of wounded men could be clearly heard. For several minutes there was no motion as the uninjured, wounded, and dead lay together in the road. The group around the gun had been the main target of the attack, and a steady hour of firing, frantically attempting to stave off disaster had exhausted the men who were still able to stand. Basinger and his gunners sagged against the high wheels of the little six-pounder, grimed from the black powder and blood-soaked from dragging back the bodies of the crew as they were struck down. The four-foot iron barrel was hotter than a chimney in hell and the stink of sulphur was in the air.

Lying in the trail just north and west of the pond, Ransom Clarke, unwounded, clutched his musket and took stock of their situation. He could see Captain Gardiner still on his feet and wondered what miracle had so far preserved the two of them. Outside the path of the road he could see nothing except waist-high grass, tall pine trees, and small oaks. Somewhere out there were Seminoles—a thousand of them to judge by the firing—and with all the luck in the world they weren't going to be able to hold out for long. If there was anything to be tried they'd better be at it. Other men were moving and Clarke saw that the captain was motioning some of them forward to bring in the wounded men and the weapons of the dead. He and eleven others, mostly wounded, made their way up the road, stooping over to keep out of sight below the grass. Quickly they stripped the cartridge boxes and hand-made cartridge bags from the belts of the corpses, snatched up the muskets, and moved on.

Near the head of the column, just beyond the bodies of Fraser and Dade, a small cluster of soldiers lay tumbled together in the middle of the trail. It was the advance guard, cut down as they wheeled toward the rear to join the main body. Clarke knelt and hastily took up what weapons he could carry. His arms full, he glanced about before turning back and saw Lieutenant Mudge slumped on the ground, his back against a tree. He had been hit in the first volley but managed to crawl behind a tree and remove one glove in order to handle musket or sword. His discarded glove lay beside him. His head was bent forward on his chest and there was blood on his coat. In a heavy whisper Clarke called to him, but he made no reply. A couple of the men carried him gently back to Gardiner and the few survivors.

The captain had rallied twenty more who had survived the first attack and put them to cutting down the smaller pines with axes brought from the wagon while Basinger brought in the wounded men and discarded weapons from the rear of the column. Clarke saw Lieutenant Henderson with a musket in his right hand encouraging the men; his left arm hung broken and useless at his side. Lieutenant Keais had been brought in and was propped against a thick pine. Both his arms were broken and he had had no chance to use the small pistol in his pocket.[17] The men had bound his arms with a large handkerchief in an effort to ease his pain but now he was unconscious—helpless. To Clarke it looked like a little over thirty men still alive, even counting

17. Belton to Jones, March 25, 1836.

those like Mudge and Keais who could be no help if there was another attack. *Jesus*—thirty men to hold off a thousand Seminoles. At least there was no one waiting for *him* back at Fort Brooke.

He stood in the road loading his own musket and a couple of spares. On his left the captain had men stacking eight-inch logs[18] in a triangular breastwork, the base roughly parallel with the road, the apex pointing toward the northwest. Eager hands were piling log on log as fast as desperate men could swing an axe and down a tree. The corners were stacked with alternate logs like a split-rail fence leaving gaps between, but there was no other way and it had to do.

Clarke looked across the palmetto tops toward the slight rise of ground a thousand yards away. For the first time he could see the enemy, mostly on foot but a few on horseback. Through the trees he could catch flashes of color as they milled about, their turbans of brightly colored cotton showing clearly in the morning sunlight. The furious activity of the troops and the ring of a dozen axes biting into the rich yellow pine had attracted their attention and more and more of them were watching as the little structure took shape. To Clarke it was looking more like a cage than a wall, and he wanted no part of it—he'd take his chances outside. He stood at the base of a thick pine, one musket in his hands and the others by his side. Nothing to do now but wait.

From the hilltop Jumper watched in silence as the white men struggled with the logs. For more than a year this attack had been planned and the planning had been perfect. Nothing must be done that would jeopardize the outcome. At least two-thirds of the soldiers were dead and of the survivors over half were wounded. Perhaps this was enough. The Seminoles had suffered no more than three dead and a few wounded and it was a fair trade.[19]

18. McCall, p. 305.
19. Alligator in Sprague, p. 91.

The warriors milling around were all for renewing the fight. Too long had the white men been allowed to make the rules in a land that was never theirs. They were unwelcome guests and they had stayed too long. The words were coming in a torrent and the tone was rising in anger. Abruptly Jumper silenced them. In tribal councils he was conceded to be among the most eloquent of Seminoles, but this was no time for speeches while the soldiers were putting up defenses. That was the white man's way—talk and talk—as though if a man were given enough words he wouldn't mind the loss of everything else.

Jumper watched with satisfaction as the soldiers gathered in a small group, even bringing their wheeled gun down the road to where others were cutting trees. Perhaps while they were bunched up like this he should strike again before they spread out and became isolated targets. Surprise had been on their side with the first blow and had brought them victory, but it would be different if his warriors had to take the rest of the white men one by one. With their logs they doubtless planned a running barricade parallel with the road—the pond at their backs to prevent attack from the rear.

For a moment he could almost feel compassion for the struggling men who worked with desperate urgency to stave off the death that he and his warriors could inflict. But this was not a time for compassion. In the seasons that were gone, a few good men on both sides had tried to understand the conflict and maintain peace, but today the time for understanding was past and the simple honesty of killing must replace the handshakes and the treaties.

Watching intently, the Indian suddenly realized what the soldiers were doing. As fast as trees were cut they were stacking them two or three high, the ends together, forming a three-sided box. They were not going to spread out; they had built a box full of holes and now they were going to get in it! Even the great gun was brought just outside. The whole of the command presented a target no more than a hundred feet wide. Only the Great Spirit could have lured the foolish soldiers into a trap like this. He would not ignore it. Immediately he gave the signal and the entire band moved boldly down the hill.[20]

Ransom Clarke watched them come. This would be the end of it and there was nothing a man could do except to fire, load, and fire again until he ran out of cartridges or time. The Seminoles were within a long musket shot of the enclosure and he could see the drooping feathers stuck in the headcloth of the leader, his long shirt, and deerskin leggings. Above a broad face with high cheekbones and small eyes, his jet black hair was stiff as wire and greased with rancid fat. Clarke swallowed hard and hoped he could stay on his feet till they came within range.

They spread out on both sides and in a moment had completely encircled the command. Now the killing began in earnest. To Clarke they looked "like devils, yelling and whooping in such a manner that the reports of the rifles were scarcely perceptible. . . ."[21] One came closer and Clarke fired, immediately dropping his musket to grab another. With rough palm behind the engraved spread eagle on the steel lock plate and hooked finger on a stiff trigger he waited for others to move in, glancing toward the enclosure and drawing confidence from the men there who seemed "cool as if they were in the woods shooting game."[22] Everyone inside had dropped down behind the loose framework of logs and those who had been felling trees had dropped their axes and scrambled inside to grab a musket and flop on their bellies.

Suddenly he felt something strike his right arm and he

20. The position and moves of the Seminoles here described are based upon both Alligator's statement in Sprague, pp. 90-91, and the details related by the white survivors, principally Clarke. The thoughts and motives of Jumper and his men are, however, assumptions made by the author, based upon every fact that could be found, leavened with reason, logic, and common sense. Others might well have drawn different conclusions.

21. Charles H. Coe, *Red Patriots* (Cincinnati, 1898), p. 61.

22. Coe, *Red Patriots*, p. 61.

grabbed at it instinctively, squeezing the wool sleeve around the hurt. He brought his hand away to steady the long musket and the blood was thick between his fingers. He pressed against the tree, firing at a dark face that slipped from sight. Another shot struck him a glancing blow on the right temple. Around him men were falling, but there was nothing he could do except to keep firing and hold back the black-haired devils. The six-pounder was punctuating the scream-filled air with periodic bursts and he wondered vaguely why it was happening. He was sure it was doing no damage but maybe the noise itself would frighten these savages. Then he forgot the noise and the savages too as a third shot struck him, going clean through one thigh and bringing him to his knees. Through the pain and fear he knew that he must get inside the barricade, for here he would die alone and quickly. When it came to hand-to-hand at the end, he wouldn't have a chance with only one good leg. He left his muskets—there'd be plenty of spares inside—and with the wounded leg dragging he crawled past the heaped bodies around the gun and into the enclosure. For a moment he sat and tried to fight off the dizziness and pain. He could see Wilson kneeling by the breastwork and other men lying among the bodies of the dead, still firing with single-minded intensity. He found a musket and joined them.

The Indians were concentrating their fire on the cannoneers. The crew was completely exposed, but with the trained habits of artillerymen they remained faithful to the piece they served. At best they could fire two rounds a minute[23] and it was a toss-up whether they would run out of cannonballs first or cannoneers. The carriage box had held fifty rounds and, until those remaining were exhausted, Gardiner and Basinger were determined that the gun would not be silenced. The few riflemen outside the breastwork did their best to cover the crew, but the range

23. Personal letter from Albert Manucy, author of *Artillery Through the Ages,* to the author, February 6, 1968.

was great and steadily the fallen artillerymen must be pushed aside for others to take their places. With each blasting paroxysm the heavy carriage bucked and rolled while another ball hurtled across the underbrush to smash a silent pine. As needles showered down, uninjured Seminoles rose above the grass, took aim, and fired. Their aim was poor, but they were six to one and it didn't matter.

Lieutenant Henderson was on one knee among the men, his musket resting on the barricade and he was loading and shooting slowly with one arm. Captain Gardiner was still on his feet, an indomitable figure in the midst of death, sword drawn and spurring hopeless men with curses of encouragement. John Keais was propped against one of three trees standing within the meager fortress, head bowed and broken arms bound and crossed as though in solemn sleep. He was unconscious and he was dying.

Kneeling behind another tree with two double-barreled shotguns, Dr. Gatlin worked carefully, dealing in death as methodically as he had dealt with life, ignoring the chilling battle cries of the Indians with the same stoicism that he turned to the wounded men around him. Life here could only be bought with death beyond the barrier and he continued to administer it, two doses at a time.

The sharp crack of rifles and the boom of muskets were sending lead into the outside of the barricade with a steady smacking sound, the odor of pine sap mingling with the acid smell of black powder. Less frequently now the soldiers' muskets boomed out, for broken limbs and bleeding bodies were slower to respond as the hours passed. Fifty men had been lost in the first volley; ten more in the first hour; thirty had manned the breastworks; now the remnant dropped more slowly, one by one.[24] Ammunition and time were running out together. Basinger, almost alone, still held to his six-pounder, but even artillerymen no longer rushed to this post of deliberate death. With resolute determination, Captain Gardiner assured them that they would fall

24. Boyd, *Florida Aflame,* pp. 92, 94.

in the discharge of their duty—or by his hand[25]—and the cannon roared out again. The last ball was finally placed when, as though at the utter futility of the effort, the match went out. As though relieved from a spell, Basinger and his men turned and entered the redoubt.

John Gatlin had stationed himself against the barricade. His powder was nearly gone. He loaded both of his double-barreled weapons, commented, "Well, I've got four barrels for them,"[26] and was cut down before he could squeeze the triggers.

Supporting his exhausted frame against a tree, Captain Gardiner still struggled to load a musket, his seemingly charmed life already cut to mortal measure by four lead balls. Vision fading and strength gone, he called out: "I can give you no more orders, my lads, do your best."[27] Another shot struck him in the chest, he stepped back one pace and fell.[28]

Only Basinger and a few men struggled on. He spoke, and his voice was steady. "I'm the only officer left, boys—let's do the best we can."[29] He swayed as he stood behind the men, his tall figure sagging with weariness. This nightmare in the woods seemed to go on and on but somehow he must keep the guns firing. Near his feet, propped on one elbow, he saw Private Clarke, one side of his face covered with blood, still reaching for muskets that had fallen about him. He thought he should say something to this steadfast trooper, and then Clarke took his fourth wound, the bullet entering the top of his right shoulder and penetrating one lung. Basinger saw blood gush from his mouth, his fingers slip off his weapon; he rolled on his face, lay still.

25. "From the report of the sole survivor of that awful scene . . ." (presumably Clarke) quoted in a statement in the Gardiner file. This statement and others are made in support of an application for pension by the widow Mrs. Gardiner.

26. Clarke in the Portland *Daily Advertiser* (date unknown), quoted in "Personal Reminiscences," p. 75.

27. *Ibid.*

28. Cullum, p. 131.

29. Potter, p. 106.

Lieutenant Basinger stood for a moment more. Then a final shot struck him, passed through both thighs and a streak of blood ran down each trouser leg like a red stripe of rank. Unconscious, he collapsed on the bodies of his men.[30]

Safely now, but with caution, the victors approached the barricade. The only sounds were stealthy footsteps and the moaning of men with fearful wounds. The old chief Micanopy halted the warriors a few yards from the bullet-scarred logs. From inside, Ransom Clarke watched them through a haze of blood. He had surfaced in a sea of pain and was staring between the logs with a fixed gaze of shock. The heavy, dark-skinned leader was speaking to the others and pointing toward the enclosure. He was stripped to the waist and his chest was daubed with red.

Clarke turned his head slowly. Someone had moved—had spoken to him. Then he saw Lieutenant Basinger a few feet away, and he seemed to be telling him something—to lie still, to play dead.[31] That wouldn't be hard.

Led by Micanopy, with Jumper and Alligator, the Indians advanced to the pen and surveyed the destruction. Jumper and another man, his cousin, stepped carefully inside between the bodies, stretched with striking regularity parallel to one another, their heads next to the logs over which they had delivered their last fire.[32] The Seminoles walked about carefully, quietly stripping off accouterments and picking up weapons but offering no indignities to the brave but vanquished enemy. Alligator and a few of the warriors followed.

Outside the north wall other warriors milled around the silent gun, pushing aside the hill of bodies to reach the cannon. Using the axes of the soldiers, they forced up the clamps that held the trunnions and lifted the barrel free of the carriage. With the confidence of their overwhelming

30. Cullum, p. 361.
31. "Personal Reminiscences," p. 74.
32. Potter, p. 138.

victory, ready hands grasped the still-hot barrel and carried it east to the lake. In the confusion of the moment, while the sturdy barrel was swung out and dropped and waves washed the thick reeds near the shore, no one noticed Private Joseph Sprague as he lay in the muck of the lake with a shattered arm, only his face breaking the surface as he struggled to breathe, undiscovered.[33]

As Jumper and his warriors moved about within the log enclosure, a figure suddenly rose up, smeared with blood and yellow teeth bared in a soundless shout. His rising from the dead transfixed the intruders and while they stared he snatched a rifle from the hand of Jumper's cousin and in a single motion swung it up by the long barrel and back down across the black-haired skull of the Indian. The heavy butt-plate drove through bone and brains, the momentum sprawling the body into the sand. Dropping the gun, Joseph Wilson, musician, leaped the north wall and ran for his life. Two of the Seminoles who had watched the scene from horseback kicked their mounts into motion and, circling around him, cut off his retreat. Keeping at a distance from this fierce apparition and wondering at his bravery, they shot him down.[34]

In a little while the weapons had been gathered and the Indians left the silent enclosure, passing back through the woods toward the west, taking their three dead with them.

Fate left little time for intermission before the final dreadful scene. Nearly fifty Negroes, runaway slaves and confederates of the Seminoles, reined in and slid to the ground from saddleless horses. White eyes rolling in dark faces, they leaned on the barricade and saw for the first time, white masters at their mercy. Escaped from brutal owners and stripped of everything but hate, they heard with pleasure the sounds of dying white men. Taking up the

33. Albert Hubbard Roberts, "The Dade Massacre," *FHQ*, V (January, 1927), p. 126.
34. Alligator's statement in Sprague, p. 91.

fallen axes of the work crew and drawing the assorted knives they carried they scrambled into the pen, cutting and hacking their way from man to man. Every throat that moaned was cut, and every heart that beat was stabbed.[35]

William Basinger, alive and conscious, lay still until he could wait no longer. On bleeding legs he rose among them and asked that his life be spared. The derisive shouts rang louder, for here was a fine prize—and with an axe they cut him down.

The killing and looting of the bodies went on, with frequent cries of "What have you got to sell?" Two negroes stopped by the body of Ransom Clarke, rolled him over on his back and stripped him of boots and coat. Faintly conscious, he heard them arguing. One wanted to bayonet him but the other stopped him saying that it was better to let him die slowly, as he surely would, for there were four lead balls in his body and his head was caked with blood. As a last vicious gesture they shot him through the shoulder. He didn't move.[36]

One by one the scavengers gathered up their prizes and hurried away. In the cold blue sky the first vulture circled slowly.

General Wiley Thompson and Lieutenant Constantine Smith strolled out of Fort King by the north gate. They had completed an early dinner and with cigars alight, they set out on a short constitutional down the road toward Mr. Rogers' store. It was chilly but clear and the sun was bright in the western sky. They passed the agency office and continued toward the log structure of the sutler, set on a low hilltop against the deep green backdrop of a heavy palmetto thicket. The cool air was invigorating and the close-cropped open land was parklike, all set about in pines. Deep in conversation they halted. They were less than two hundred yards from the sutler's place.

35. *Ibid.*; Clarke in "Personal Reminiscences" (also for Basinger's death), pp. 74, 75; Potter, p. 106.
36. Boyd, *Florida Aflame,* p. 93.

For Osceola the moment had come. Clear-eyed, he sighted down the barrel of his expensive rifle.[37] Through the screen of fronds he could see his "friend," the man who had locked him in a cage. He caught his breath in satisfaction—and slowly, slowly, he squeezed. The crash of his weapon was followed by a dozen echoes as the men around him fired their rifles in ragged chorus, and Wiley Thompson was knocked off his feet by the impact of one pound of lead. Then Osceola was on his feet and running, the rifle in his left hand and a knife in his right while the shouts of his warriors split the air. For a moment he stood over the body, savoring the sight of the dead man, then he knelt and drove the long blade deep in the right breast of the blood-soaked shirt.[38] His warriors had encircled the house where the sutler and four others had been eating, but Osceola paid no attention to the shrill war cries or the blasting of rifles as they cut down their victims. With complete concentration he grasped the gray hair of the agent, pulling his head upright to circle the scalp with shallow, efficient strokes and peeling away the cap of hair and skin. With the thin gray strands twisted in his fingers he gave a final tug and it was done, the naked bloody head falling back on the sand. Without a backward glance at the sprawled and mutilated thing he turned and joined his men.[39]

Four men and a boy lay dead around the table. A few servants had escaped through the windows and now it was relatively quiet. Scalps were being taken from the four men while other warriors prowled through the house searching

37. Cohen, p. 69. No statement was ever made by Osceola or other Seminoles (to the author's knowledge) that this rifle was the same one given him by the agent. Yet it seems likely that Osceola would have employed his best weapon in this important and fateful act and the author has accepted this assumption.

38. Harris to Gibson, December 30, 1835, in Boyd, *Florida Aflame*, p. 71, "[the body] of General Thompson was perforated with *fourteen bullets*, and a deep knife wound in the right breast [and was] scalped."

39. There was no white eye-witness to the killing of Thompson. Osceola was seen and heard among the Seminoles at the time, however, and circumstances being what they were between Osceola and the agent, it seems reasonable to assume that the event occurred as described.

vainly for plunder. All the stores had been removed to the fort and the place was empty.

The surprise of the attack had been complete and so quickly over that not a soldier had yet emerged from the fort. Osceola summoned his men with a final, defiant cry, and together they returned as they had come, into the palmetto and beyond.[40]

Forty miles to the south, a blood-soaked slaughter pen stood beside the Fort King Road. The carriage of the little six-pounder still smouldered in the darkness. The torch put to the carriage had spread to the tall grass, and now scorched earth surrounded the last redoubt and the smell of burnt vegetation smothered the odor of death.[41] In the western sky a broken moon was waning. Inside the pen faithful soldiers still knelt or lay stretched full length along the low walls, faces to the foe. Many rested their heads on the upper log of the little fort like toy soldiers abandoned by a child.[42]

Gold watches in the pockets of dead officers ticked on. It was nine o'clock when the voice of a soul in torment croaked from parched lips that barely moved.[43] Bewildered eyes stared up from between lids that were crusted with dirt and blood and a melancholy moon looked down on Ransom Clarke. He lay on his back and saw moss beards waving gently from pine limbs against a deep blue sky. Through pain and shock his brain tried to catch hold of reality, stumbled, tried again. It needed oxygen and the

40. Harris to Gibson, December 30, 1835, in Boyd, *Florida Aflame*, p. 71.

41. Both Clarke and Joseph Sprague, quoted in "Personal Reminiscences," p. 75, state that a fire was set by the Negroes—beginning with the cart, according to Clarke, while Sprague thought it was the gun carriage. The author has accepted Sprague in this case, for it seems that the carriage for the hated cannon would be a more likely target for such vengeance than a mere supply wagon. The fact of a fire (between the time of battle and Gaines' arrival) is clearly attested by many in Gaines' army: Hitchcock to Gaines, February 22, 1836; Potter, p. 138; Duncan, February 20, 1836. The time of it would appear to have been more likely as stated in the text rather than spontaneous combustion during the weeks that followed.

42. McCall, pp. 305-6.

43. "Personal Reminiscences," p. 75.

punctured lung had cut the supply by half. Consciousness came and went like waves from an invisible sea, his mind slowly gathering scenes and events and patching them into a terrible but workable memory. There had been a battle—it must have lasted for hours, but everything was as still as death and it had to be over. He needed water—he could hardly swallow—he wanted someone to bring the water and he tried to call, but no one answered. He had to get up—rouse the others—why did they sleep when the Indians might return—crazy fools—got to get up—water, water. He tried to move his head. It made him dizzy and conciousness nearly slipped away. He forced the dark waves back and tried again. Was that the lieutenant? He'd been alive a few minutes ago—no, it must have been hours—but it was a big man that lay nearby—he could see his black beard and his blue frock coat and he was sprawled like a broken doll. The dark blots must be blood. But what about the others? Forcing his fright into anger he lurched up on his side to curse them into life, and before he fainted he knew that the arm on which he leaned was broken.

In fevered dreams he struggled to consciousness and savagely grabbed a breath of air while bulging eyes stared again through gummy lids. It was night, but hard ground filled his clutching fingers and then the thirst returned. Slowly then, with caution, he rolled to his left side working with unwounded arm and leg while the broken right arm hung unnaturally across his chest, the shoulder sagging in from a broken clavicle. He took no time to nurse the shattered bones and torn flesh, for he *must* have water. He managed to raise himself on his left knee and hand, the right leg, throbbing and bloody from the bullet in his thigh, serving as additional support while he moved like a crippled dog about the enclosure, gasping in anger and pain, searching out each canteen that still lay about and licking hungrily after each drop until the thirst was gone.[44]

44. Clarke's condition at this time is an assumption by the author based upon discussion of his wounds with competent medical authorities.

He rested, summoning strength from the water, staring in dreadful fascination at the men slumped all about him, their dead eyes glowing like pearls in the moonlight. Most of them were along the north and west faces of the breastwork, including Lieutenant Basinger, and near him, Henderson and Keais. Many men had been left undisturbed by the victors after the battle, but here and there a skull had been crushed, or a scalp taken by the Negroes, while all muskets and ammunition boxes were gone. The naked upper bodies of those men whose coats and shirts had been taken by the Negroes were startlingly white, their limbs "marking the agony with which life ceased." [45]

As he lurched into motion, coatless and barefooted, he had no clear idea in his pain-fogged brain except that he must get moving—must head back down the long road to Tampa Bay. It was farther than Fort King but it was less likely to be barred by Indians and there was just a chance that he might be found by the long-delayed command of Major Mountfort. He took no thought for medicines or laudanum that might be in Dr. Gatlin's kit, for boots or clothing that might be taken from a trooper who no longer needed them, not even for food that might have been overlooked in the mess chests of the officers. Bootless, bleeding, and empty-bellied he started out.

He crawled between and over the bodies toward the rude barricade, hardly conscious of the chill that had settled over the once-warm skin and the stiffness of death that held the bodies awkwardly even when he had to drag himself across them. He tried to balance on his left hand and knee again, bracing himself with the broken arm on the right and it was hopeless, but he didn't know it. There were at least thirty men within the enclosure and there was no way to avoid crawling across those who lay together by the wall. In shock, and only partly lucid, he had no thought for the horror of it—and then he laid his hand on bare flesh that was at least as warm as his own.

45. Belton to Jones, March 25, 1836.

It took several moments for his mind to register and react to the message from his senses. He scrambled back, desperate in his eagerness, sitting down to free his good hand for shaking and slapping at this man who lived. Suddenly the terror of his loneliness in a box of dead men became unbearable as he began to understand that there was a chance he might not be alone. He crouched over the limp form like a goblin, peering at the face and demanding that it wake up. The chest was moving and he knew the man was still alive. Then the lips moved and the eyes opened. The face was ghostly in the pale light but as animation returned he recognized him as Ed De Courcy of his own B Company, Second Regiment.

Blond hair lay across a pale forehead. Blue eyes dragged open. Wounds in his left arm and side were not serious.[46] Somehow he had escaped the butchery and he quickly got his bearings at the frantic urging of Ransom Clarke, who raved obscenely of the Devil's luck that had brought them to this condition.[47] Clarke insisted that they must be on their way—the Seminoles or the Negroes might return—and survival depended on their reaching help. De Courcy, suffering from shock and his own wounds, couldn't understand how Clarke meant to get back to Fort Brooke, a full sixty miles away; but there was no resisting his insistent demands. He got to his feet; Clarke was already making his agonized way over the logs. Dazed and staggering, De Courcy tried to help the more seriously wounded man over; then, supporting him so that he could hobble along, they made painful, shuffling progress away from the enclosure that held the nightmare.

Outside, death had set another scene, but on a larger scale. Up and down the road lay the bodies of some seventy men, along with the oxen and horses and scattered around them all, as if to balance the picture, were smashed cartridge boxes, fragments of clothing, and here and there a shoe or

46. Boynton, p. 293.
47. Bemrose, p. 65.

an old straw hat which had been exchanged for a military cap.[48] In their stumbling passage, the two men passed the partly burnt remains of the supply wagon with the oxen still yoked lying dead near it. But a thousand dead would have meant little to them in their confused and semi-conscious state. Over the bodies and past them they stumbled on, clinging to each other like lost souls and muttering their torment. They had come this far through impossible odds and though broken and bleeding, they must go on.

So the proud little command that had sallied forth to drum and fife to challenge the power of a barbaric people had lost. Their bright sashes and gold buttons would dull and tarnish in the sun and rain of days to come. Only these two forlorn men, and later Joseph Sprague, could leave the field, while the victors with their brilliant chief Osceola gathered on an island in the Great Swamp, hung the scalps of officers and men on a ten foot pole "around which they exultingly danced till daylight, accompanying their frantic mirth by songs ridiculing and defying the white men."[49] But their victory chant was premature; the old, free way of life was doomed long before.

This was only the first battle of a seven year war-to-come, but on a single stage it presented a preview of the boldness, savagery, and determination that forecast the outcome. Settlers and soldiers alike would continue to probe and push, in weakness and in strength; the Seminoles, with native intuition, would strike and strike again—not because they hoped ever to annihilate the advance guard of civilization, but in an effort to destroy the will of a more numerous nation and thereby retain the freedom of a simple way of life. But, like Clarke and De Courcy, these white men of America could fight and lose, yet as long as one survived he would crawl away if need be to lick his wounds, only to return—and this time he would conquer. He would never give up.

48. Potter, p. 138.
49. Sprague, p. 91.

EPILOGUE

Through the long night and into the morning of the following day Ransom Clarke and Edwin De Courcy made their halting way, resting often but always rising again to push on. Clarke's moments of clarity were often broken by bewilderment and then delirium. De Courcy helped him through the worst times, supporting the taller, more seriously wounded man, grateful for Clarke's presence on a lonely road, slowing his own progress to that of his companion. Often Clarke would have to drop to his knees when the wounded thigh became too painful and in this position he would crawl, stopping only when exhaustion and pain made it impossible to continue. He slipped in and out of consciousness while the moments of rest lowered the level

157

of agony when De Courcy would pull him to his feet again and they would stumble on, accompanied by the threnody of Clarke's terrible and continual cursing.

By noon they had been traveling for the better part of twelve hours and had put many miles behind them. They were almost asleep on their feet when an Indian on horseback traveling up the road toward them put his mount into a gallop. Instinctively they separated, De Courcy running off to the left of the road and Clarke scrambling to the right, each hoping he might conceal himself in the brush and throw the warrior off his trail. The Indian dashed up, a rifle in his hand, and wheeled his horse into the underbrush. In a few moments he found one of the men, and the crash of his rifle hung in the air. Leaping down, the Indian slashed the forehead, tearing off the scalp and leaving the soldier slumped in a bloody heap beneath the palmettos. Remounting, he beat through the hammock searching for the other man who, at one point, was only ten feet away and could see the blood-smeared legs of the rider. But the Indian was in a hurry and soon the sound of hooves pounding up the road toward the north reached the terrified listener hidden within a thick growth of palmetto. More dead than alive, Ransom Clarke sank into exhausted sleep.[1]

On the afternoon of the same day, some fifty miles to the south and while a survivor of the battle that would become known as Dade's Massacre huddled in cold and hungry sleep, word was brought to Captain Francis Belton at Fort Brooke that an injured man was approaching on the Fort King Road. The soldier was Private John Thomas.[2] He explained the injury to his back "while assisting to lift . . . (the) six pounder out of the Hillsborough River"[3] and his subsequent inability to accompany the command. After hours of rest near the Big Hillsborough he had started back, barely able to move without exquisite pain and carrying

1. Clarke in "Personal Reminiscences," pp. 75-76.
2. Belton to Jones, January 1, 1836.
3. Surgeon's Certificate for Pension in Thomas file, June 28, 1837.

only a small ration of food. It had taken nearly five days to travel the twenty-five miles back from the river, making only a few painful miles per day. He had seen only one Seminole on the road, a man to whose axe he had fitted a new handle a few days before at the fort, but had managed to buy him off with the six dollars he carried.[4] To the persistent questions of the officers he could only say that as far as he knew the command had gotten through but he had no knowledge of them since the morning of the twenty-fifth. Exhausted and suffering, he was put to bed.

On the following day, the thirtieth, the support ship bearing the camp equipage and subsistence stores for both Lieutenant Greyson's company and Major Mountfort's finally hove to off the fort and anchored in deep water. They had followed Greyson's transport into the wrong harbor and grounded, finally working themselves off and returning around Gadsden's point. The supplies were lightered off and carried to the fort against the possibility of attack.

The stockade had been greatly strengthened and additional blockhouses erected for Indian attack still seemed imminent.[5] The Seminole hostage employed as a runner and sent to Fort King had returned on December 28, two days late. He had brought a message, but not from Generals Thompson or Clinch at headquarters. The message was from the Negro Abraham and Hitchiti Mico, a chief. Derisively, they said Belton's talk was good and that he might expect them on the thirtieth.[6] They might be bluffing, but the defenses were as strong as they could be made and the men were ready. The waiting was the worst. Yet the day passed quietly and on the afternoon of December 31, New Year's Eve, another man was sighted on the Military Road. He was clad in blood and dirt and he crawled on hands and knees. He was almost too weak to curse. Beneath

4. Belton to Jones, January 1, 1836.
5. John C. Casey to Thomas Basinger (brother of Lieutenant Basinger), January 2, 1836, given in "Personal Reminiscences," Appendix III.
6. Belton to Jones, January 1, 1836.

the filth and terrible wounds he was recognized as Private Ransom Clarke and his incredible journey was over.[7]

At the hospital he gave heartbreaking answers to Belton's questions. In a remarkably coherent way he told of the attack, the battle, and the aftermath. One by one, he recounted the death of Dade, Mudge, Basinger, Gardiner, Keais, Henderson, and Gatlin. Each name fell like a blow on the circle of listeners, for none among Dade's command had been without close friends at Fort Brooke. And quickly the awful word was spread among the widows of officers and enlisted men. Husbands and fathers had been "stricken down, as if one blow had been death to all, and that blow, a bolt from heaven!"[8]

And as the old year ended, so the New Year began. On the morning of the first, the last survivor came in. This was Private Joseph Sprague of Captain Fraser's B Company, wounded in the arm. He brought the tragic note written by Fraser to Major Mountfort which he had found along the road close to their encampment of the last night. It had been stuck in a cleft stick as they crossed a dry creek bed that last morning and it stated that they were being watched, but pushing on. Sprague was able to fill in one name that Clarke had left out. He had seen Captain Fraser fall at the first fire and confirmed his death.[9]

So it was over: the plans that might have been and the lives that had tried to weight the scales against the danger threatening a far-off fort. The words of Colonel Fanning only a month before had been prophetic: "We have fallen into the error committed at the Commencement of every Indian War: The display of too little force—The attempt to do too much with inadequate means."[10] It was all over—and it was just beginning.

The same day, January 1, 1836, Captain Belton wrote a full report to the adjutant general in Washington. Writing

7. *Ibid.*
8. Belton to Jones, March 24, 1836.
9. *Ibid.*, January 1, 1836.
10. *FTP*, XXV, 201.

firmly but in sorrow, he detailed the tragedy and its aftermath. And finally: "I have ordered to embark on board the
return Transport to New Orleans, several families, made
widows and orphans by the fatal battle. . . ."[11] The transport left Fort Brooke on January 4, carrying nearly fifty
women and children.[12] Frances Basinger was so distraught
that Mrs. Heiskell, wife of the post surgeon, accompanied
her and tended her through the unusually long voyage to
New Orleans.[13] There, seventeen hundred and forty-one
dollars was quickly subscribed for their relief by the citi-
zens.[14]

From New Orleans the wives of the enlisted men found
their way as best they could back to their homes or parents,
though a few, like Ellen Kenny, stayed on with the army,
doing wash and receiving army rations in return.[15] The
officers' wives seem to have gathered by mutual consent at
the garrison at Baton Rouge where Frances Basinger
wrote that "we live in a comfortable sympathetic little
circle. . . ."[16]

Captain Belton sent his report out with Judge Steele
bound for Tallahassee, the capitol of the territory. On
January 17 Steele delivered the news to Governor Eaton and
the following day the governor forwarded it by express to
General Clinch at Fort Drane.[17] Thus it was over three
weeks after Dade's battle before Colonel Fanning, with the
general, got the news that Gardiner and the rest had been
struck down forty miles south of their goal.

And so the word traveled—slowly, growing more distorted
with each writing or telling but rousing men throughout

11. Belton to Jones, January 1, 1836.
12. Daniel F. Blanchard, *An Authentic Narrative of the Seminole War*
(Providence, 1836), p. 16.
13. Mrs. William Basinger to Mrs. Peter Basinger, March 12, 1836, given in
"Personal Reminiscences," Appendix VI.
14. Blanchard, *Authentic Narrative*, p. 16.
15. Statement by Ellen Kenny in an application for pension, found in the
Michael Kenny file, N.A.R.S.
16. Mrs. William Basinger to Mrs. Peter Basinger, March 12, 1836.
17. Boyd, *Florida Aflame*, p. 97.

the nation. In the civilian ranks of government, policy makers rose in the righteous wrath of men of honor—caught in a dishonorable act. From Andrew Jackson on down, they had endeavored unsuccessfully to effect the removal or disolution of the Seminole Nation, both within and outside the law; here now was honest cause for retaliation. Foul massacre had been done. Against such fiends every red-blooded man would take up arms. No matter that the victors had struck in daylight against well-armed soldiers; that they fought solely in defense of their land and their freedom. Forgotten now was the fact that the Indians had offered no indignity to a fallen foe or that the horror was perpetrated by those who had dealt most intimately with white men. All the inflexible (and sometimes heart-breaking) determination that had gained for the white man the mastery of a mixed world was brought to bear in what would someday be a forgotten war.

By January 15, news of the disaster was received by General Edmund Pendleton Gaines on his arrival in New Orleans where he promptly organized a force of eleven hundred men and boarded ship for Tampa Bay. After a week's passage they landed, bringing to an end the threat of attack on Fort Brooke, and were ready to complete Major Dade's relief expedition to Fort King and to reinforce General Clinch. From Ransom Clarke, Gaines and his staff heard the details of the battle and Clarke, somewhat subdued now by the rank of his listeners, related the story in a simple, quiet way that carried the conviction of truth.[18]

On the morning of February 20, fifty-four days after the battle, this army of eleven hundred reached the battleground. Lieutenant James Duncan wrote: "Gracious God what a sight! The vultures rose in clouds as the approach of the column drove them from their prey[.] [T]he very breastwork was black with them[.] [S]ome hovered over us as we looked upon the scene before us whilst others settled upon the adjoining trees waiting for

18. McCall, p. 307.

our departure, in order again to return to their prey. The interior of the breastwork was covered with the bodies of the slain, as they had been left by their savage foe . . . the bodies of all the officers were identified, and many of the soldiers."[19]

Belton, Mountfort, Alvord, McCall, and Dr. Heiskell were among the personal friends of the officers of Dade's command who were in this larger army[20] that was the first to follow in their footsteps through the Nation. And another member of the group was the incredible Ransom Clarke who, only partially recovered, had volunteered to join the return trip.[21] The terrible scene of desolation matched in nearly every particular the events that Clarke had described and which as Major Belton stated, "a melancholy imagination had often depicted."[22]

Lieutenant McCall had long served with Major Dade and readily recognized his body, still lying in the road where it had fallen at the first fire. "The flesh had shrunk, but the skin had remained whole, dried, smooth, and hard; the hair and beard remained. . . ." He was much affected by the tragic scene and felt that "the picture of those brave men lying thus in their 'sky-blue' clothing, which had scarcely faded, was such as can never be effaced from my memory."[23]

Dr. Heiskell gathered the last effects of William Basinger —a large silk handkerchief, some letters, a red leather money belt that was strapped about his waist, a white net undershirt, and a lock of his hair.[24]

Captain Belton moved among the bodies helping to identify them before burial. A grave for the remains of the officers was being dug just outside the enclosure on the east and as the body of John Keais was moved his small pocket pistol, overlooked by the Negroes, fell to the ground and was retrieved by Belton. Gold and silver coins were gathered

19. Duncan, entry for February 20, 1836.
20. Potter, p. 133.
21. McCall, p. 306.
22. Belton to Jones, March 25, 1836.   23. McCall, p. 305.
24. Mrs. William Basinger to Mrs. Peter Basinger, March 12, 1836.

from the bodies, as well as breastpins, watches, and rings for delivery to relatives. Hundreds of dollars in paper money were found scattered about, some of them partly burned from the brush fire which had swept the area after the battle.[25] James Duncan carefully examined the entire location and had the presence of mind to sketch a map of the site in his diary, while another map was made on the spot by Woodburne Potter, a staff officer.[26]

After identification and removal of the bodies from the breastwork, two large graves were dug within the low walls, each thirteen feet long, five feet wide, and four feet deep.[27] Here the enlisted men were laid to rest while the remains of the officers were placed in their separate grave, the dissolute bodies still clothed in the remnants of their uniforms. In his official report, Captain Belton seemed to address himself directly to his fallen comrades, "Your agonized limbs were decently adjusted by affection's unrevolting hands, and with reverence, as if your spirits were around—and although the pomp of the Soldiers laurelled here, was absent, yet sympathy mourned and sorrow wept. . . ."[28] The six-pounder, brought from the pond, was placed muzzle-down on the grave, and then the troops were drawn up in a column of companies led by the immediate friends of the deceased officers. With the full band of the Fourth Regiment of Infantry playing "Bruce's Address," a mournful Scottish dirge, the two columns moved in opposite directions with reversed arms three times around the graves in cadenced step. The ceremony was closed with the playing of the "Dead March."[29]

25. Duncan, entry for February 20, 1836.

26. Both of these maps, with another made in January, 1837, by Lieutenant Edwin Rose and a fourth by an unknown author were submitted to Adjutant General Jones by Belton on March 25, 1836. All but Rose's show strong indications of having been based on a common sketch, a not unlikely circumstance, and all portray the battle site and general surroundings much as they look today.

27. Measurements were determined during excavation of the grave in March, 1964.

28. Belton to Jones, March 25, 1836.

29. Duncan, entry for February 20, 1836; Belton to Jones, March 25, 1836; Potter, p. 138-39; McCall, p. 315.

For seven years the bodies of the command rested peacefully beneath the pines and oaks along the Fort King Road while the war their deaths had forced flared and crashed across the territory. Then, in the summer of 1842, a subscription was raised among all officers and men serving in Florida, each one donating one day's pay with the total to be spent erecting a "sufficient but unostentatious memorial" in the garden at St. Francis Barracks in St. Augustine.[30] During July, the quiet of Dade's battleground was broken by the arrival of the wagons and the men who took up the bodies of Major Dade and his command, shoveled the dirt back over the gold and silver buttons that had adorned them and the lead balls that had killed them and, with the remains in two wagons, returned to St. Augustine.[31] On Monday, August 15, they were deposited in three vaults with full military honors.[32] Nine days later the headquarters of the military department at Cedar Key announced: "hostilities with the Indians within this Territory have ceased. . . ."[33] The Second Seminole War was over.

30. Circular signed by Assistant Adjutant General S. Cooper, June 13, 1842, given in *Record of Officers*, p. 10.
31. Cooper to Isaac V. D. Reeve, June 6, 1842, N.A.R.S.
32. Order No. 25, S. Cooper, July 25, 1842, in Sprague, p. 522.
33. Order No. 28, S. Cooper, August 24, 1842, in *Record of Officers*, p. 11.

OFFICERS AND MEN

T HE SEEMINGLY indestructible Ransom Clarke was evidently the first of the three white survivors of Dade's command to die, though in an interview published in the *Daily National Intelligencer* (Washington, D.C.) on June 14, 1837, he stated: "They [Thomas and Sprague] joined another expedition, two months after [the massacre], but before their wounds were healed, and they soon died of them." Doubtless the expedition he refers to was that of General Gaines which left Fort Brooke for the battleground on February 13, an expedition of which Clarke himself was a member. None of the men who were with Gaines and who later wrote of their experiences mention either of the men, though McCall states clearly that Clarke *was* with them. It seems to follow, then, that mention would have been made of Thomas or Sprague if they were also in the company, though this is only conjecture. However, Clarke was clearly mistaken in assuming them dead in 1837, since they can each be traced beyond that date.

Except for the expedition with Gaines, Clarke is believed to have spent the rest of his army service at Fort Brooke, probably receiving medical care, since one source mentions during the spring of 1836 that he was among a great number of sick in the fort.[1] On May 2 he received his discharge there

1. Captain James Barr, *A Correct and Authentic Narrative of the Indian War in Florida* (New York, J. Narine, 1836), p. 9, written in semi-diary form with this mention under date of March 16, 1836.

(though his enlistment would not be up until August 9) and left for Washington, D.C., via New Orleans, arriving in June, 1836. He was granted a pension for total disability and by September had begun receiving payments of eight dollars a month.[2] It must be assumed that his condition, both physically and financially, was on the bare edge of survival for even in 1836 his income could hardly be called comfortable. As for his wounds, the shoulder that had been smashed with two lead balls never healed and continued to discharge fragments of bone. He quite possibly retained at least a limp from the thigh wound, and probably he had to get by with the services of only one lung. However, Clarke was not a man to be easily downed, and in 1838 he met and married, in Albany, New York, Miss Eunice Luceba French.

Perhaps because of the increased need for income Clarke began giving lectures about this time, charging twelve and one-half cents admission fee to hear his account of his capture by the Seminoles, how he was "held in captivity *eight months;* escaped by killing *seven Indians* who were left to guard him. . . ."[3]

That the account was somewhat embroidered seems clear, but the audiences must have been jaded, indeed, if any embroidery on his adventures was needed. On August 24, 1839, Eunice presented him with a daughter whom they named Caroline,[4] and this year, too, he published a long pamphlet titled *Narrative of Ransom Clarke* which was evidently an elaboration of his lecture material.

But the terrible wounds he had sustained in the battle of which he talked and wrote finally overcame even his iron resistance and in 1840, on November 18, Ransom Clarke was dead. The long and dreadful journey that had begun at Fort Brooke, on Tampa Bay, Florida, ended in a snow-covered grave in Greigsville, Livingston County, New York.

2. Boyd, *Florida Aflame,* pp. 90-91; application for bounty land by Eunice Clarke, August 30, 1854, in Clinton County, N.Y.
3. Broadside found in Clarke file, N.A.R.S.
4. Application for bounty land by Eunice Clarke.

Into twenty-eight years he had packed a lifetime of adventure but now he was home for good.[5]

John Thomas, "a quiet, staid man . . . respected by all,"[6] was sent north to Fort Drane after a partial recovery from his back injury. Here he served as hospital attendant for a time, going about his work quietly and seldom if ever speaking of the massacre which he had avoided by the intervention of a lenient, if painful, providence. Dr. Weightman examined him in St. Augustine in May, 1837, and declared him "Three fourths disabled from obtaining his subsistence."[7] A month later, on June 28, he was discharged at Picolata and the next month was granted a pension of six dollars per month, payable twice a year at Boston, Massachusetts, which he listed as his intended residence.

Nothing is known of his life for the next forty-five years until early in the year 1883 when a Mr. Clark (no relation to Ransom) of Volga City, Iowa, wrote to the Commissioner of Pensions in Washington to ask if a pension had been granted Thomas "as he is a very old man [82] and very poor, depending on charity at the poor house for support."[8]

So far, no further trace has been found of the only white octogenarian survivor of the command of Major Dade. It can be presumed that he died before the end of the decade.

And Joseph Sprague. After recovering from his wounds he was transferred to Company H where he served until the expiration of his enlistment on August 22, 1836, and

5. D.A.R., *Cemetery, Church, and Town Records*, XXIV, 42, supplied by Manuscripts and History Section, the University of the State of New York; file of marked graves of Livingston County before 1885 in the office of County Historian, Genesee, New York.

6. Bemrose, p. 72.

7. Surgeon's Certificate for Pension, Thomas file.

8. Certainly there is a possibility that this John Thomas is not the Thomas of the massacre, but our assumption here is based upon two points: the letter requesting information concerning a pension is in and a part of the file of Thomas of the massacre, placed there (rather than in another of a probable profusion of John Thomases on file) in some confidence by members of the N.A.R.S. and also, with the inquiry itself it is made clear that the subject of the letter did serve as early as the Black Hawk War, and hence, *could* have been the Thomas of the massacre.

was discharged at Micanopy, Florida. Less than three months later he was in Sackett's Harbor, New York, where he re-enlisted for the fifth time, being assigned to the Second Infantry Regiment. Nothing is known of this tour of duty except that he served his full three years and was discharged for the last time on November 12, 1839. At thirty-six years of age he walked out of the gates of Fort Gilmer, Georgia, and into the ranks of the lost people of the past.

The remarkable Negro Louis Pacheco was for a time assumed to have been buried with the rest of Dade's command, but in the early summer of 1837, at Fort Brooke, Captain John Charles Casey, the officer who had hired him as interpreter for Major Dade, looked up from his desk to see Pacheco standing before him.[9] As slave property of the Indians he had come in with them in accordance with the abortive "Treaty of Fort Dade," signed on March 6, 1837, by which the Second Seminole War had theoretically ended and the Indians agreed to removal.[10]

According to Jumper, who accompanied Pacheco to Fort Brooke, the slave's life had been spared during and after the battle by Jumper's order and Pacheco therefore belonged to him. The first volley on that fateful morning had missed Pacheco, but with great presence of mind he had immediately dropped to the ground and simulated death. With Major Dade and the advance guard lying dead just in front of him and the Seminoles approaching during the first attack, he had gotten to his feet and pleaded for his life, explaining that he was a slave and had accompanied the command against his will.[11]

Jumper's story was accepted by the military authorities and Pacheco was sent west with a group of Seminoles. He continued on to the new Indian Nation in Oklahoma Territory where he lived on an equal footing with the Indians.

9. McKay, II, 481.

10. Frank Laumer, "This Was Fort Dade," *FHQ,* XLV (July, 1966), 11.

11. Statement by Pacheco in the Austin, Texas, *Commercial Journal,* August, 1861, quoted in McKay, II, 480-81.

170

MASSACRE!

Later he was sold again and taken to Austin, Texas, where he lived for forty years. Presumably he gained his freedom during these years though little is known of his life in Texas. He seemed to have carried with genuine fondness the memory of the southeastern country in which he was born and for the family of his early master Antonio Pacheco, for he finally made his way back to Jacksonville, Florida, in 1892, and the home of Mrs. John L'Engle, the daughter of his first master. As a young girl, she had taught him to read. Mrs. L'Engle was convinced that this ancient black man was indeed her former pupil, and here he stayed until his death in 1895, still protesting his innocence of the rumored charge that he had betrayed Major Dade and his command to the Indians.[12] The facts bear him out.

Amanda Middleton Dade and her daughter, Fannie Langhorne, returned to their residence in Pensacola to live with Mrs. Dade's father Isaac and her widowed younger sister Mary Stuart Wilkinson.[13]

It appears that Amanda had been born in 1811, married Francis Dade at the age of sixteen (he was thirty-five), and was widowed at twenty-five. She never remarried, living on in Pensacola for the greater part of her remaining life. In 1836 she was granted a pension of $300 per year but Congress refused to extend this beyond the five year expiration date when she petitioned them for relief in 1840. She applied again in 1848 and was again refused, but five years later the laws governing pensions were changed and in April, 1853, the Secretary of the Interior signed the papers granting her a pension of $300 per year "during her natural life" and retroactive to 1840, entitling her to almost $4,000 in back payments.[14]

12. McKay, II, 479-81; Boyd, *Florida Aflame*, p. 106; Porter, "Three Fighters for Freedom," pp. 65-72. At the conclusion of the Fort Brooke Post Return for December, 1835, mention is made of Dade's battle and here again Pacheco is listed as ". . . Interpreter Negro."
13. Census, Escambia County, Florida, for 1840, 1850, 1860.
14. H.R. Report No. 667 (26 Cong., 1 sess.), July 10, 1840, p. 520; H.R. Report No. 532 (30 Cong., 1 sess.), April 26, 1848.

During the intervening years while the two women helped to support themselves and their elderly father by teaching, each suffered the loss of an only child. Only three months after the death of Mary's offspring, young Fannie Dade, the daughter of Major Dade, died of tuberculosis on August 28, 1848, after a lingering and painful illness. The seventeen-year-old girl was buried in St. Michaels Cemetery just a few blocks from her parents' handsome frame house on Palafox Street.[15]

During the following decade Isaac Middleton died and the two widows were alone, though by 1860 they could list their real and personal estate at forty-five hundred dollars. Here they continued to live during the rigors of the Civil War; Amanda's last legal act was dated July, 1866, when she signed an oath to "abide by and faithfully support all laws and proclamations which have been made during the existing rebellion with reference to the emancipation of slaves: So help me God."[16] Within a year she was dead. Major Dade's widow lies buried now beside their daughter in the Middleton family plot in St. Michaels Cemetery in Pensacola, Florida.

Captain and Mrs. Gardiner had a large social acquaintance in Key West, and when word of the captain's death was received the little city went into mourning. "Captain Gardiner's wife and children were objects of tender consideration . . . and every kindness and attention possible was extended to them in their bereavement."[17] Mrs. Gardiner, whose illness almost saved her husband's life, lived on for sixty-one years after his death, dying on October 22, 1896.[18]

As to the greater number of the enlisted men who accompanied Major Dade on that ill-fated march, very little

15. Pensacola *Gazette*, September 2, 1848.
16. Dade file, N.A.R.S.
17. Jefferson B. Browne, *Key West: The Old and the New* (The Record Company, St. Augustine, 1912), p. 84.
18. Report of United States Pension Agency, Boston, in Gardiner file.

information is available. The "Registers of Enlistments" have provided basic statistics on each man (name, age, color of eyes and hair, complexion, height, place of birth, occupation, when, where, and by whom enlisted, period of enlistment, regiment and company, date of desertions, if any, and date of discharge). From personal files that were available on a few of the men we had access to personal letters and applications by widows for pensions in which many circumstances surrounding the lives of individual men were detailed. In the effort to learn more of a man than his name and shape, we found too often that only in his death had he left a mark on history, and even that was surprisingly faint.

In the case of those born in a foreign country (and almost exactly half of the enlisted men were), our letters to their birthplaces searching for some trace that they had actually lived were, for the most part, in vain. As W. A. Thorburn, Curator of the Scottish United Services Museum of Edinburgh wrote:

> The Seminole War received very little attention here, and I can find only brief and biased reference to it. . . . [They] are concerned mainly with reports of "brave Seminoles fighting for their hunting grounds" and lamentations that Britain was not in a position "to take the red men of America under its protection"—"to recompense them for the wrongs inflicted by quasi-civilized whites.
>
> The military journals were inclined to treat it as a rather objectionable affair between unspeakable Americans and poor downtrodden Indians, and it is most irritating to see so little attempt to see it from the soldier's point of view. . . . One must of course realise the world was a different place in the 1830's. . . .
>
> Little was known about the private lives or birthplaces of enlisted men, and they were . . . just names who would, had they not died in a battle, been unknown forever.[19]

19. W. A. Thorburn to Laumer, September 12, 1963.

Fort Brooke at Tampa Bay on the Gulf of Mexico.

Palmettos bordering the "round clay sink" where Dade and his men camped the night before the massacre. (Pond on the property of David Davis, Bushnell, Florida.)

MARY WATSON

"On our right and a little to our rear, was a large pond." Here wounded Joseph Sprague hid, and after the battle was able to make it back to Fort Brooke.

"We immediately began to fell trees and erect a little triangular breastwork." (Reconstruction in Dade Battlefield Historic Memorial Park.)

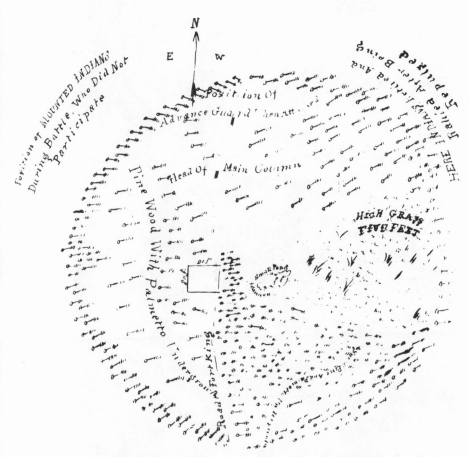

Battle Ground of Maj. DADE
7 Miles from Little WITHLACOOCHEE
Decem 28th 1835

Map which accompanied Major Belton's official report of the battle.

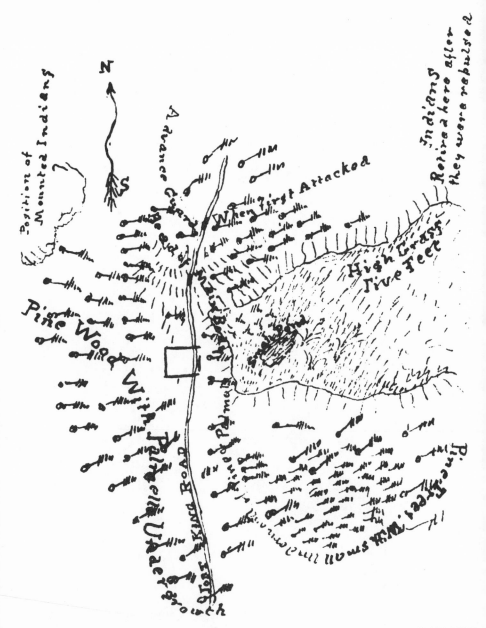

Position of Mounted Indians

N
S

Advance Gun

When first Attacked

Indians
Retired here after
they were repulsed

High Grass
Five Feet

Pine Wood With Pine Under growth

Our Kind Road

Burned Palmetto

Pine Trees With small thorny

JAMES DUNCAN, DIARY

Duncan's map, made eight weeks after the massacre.

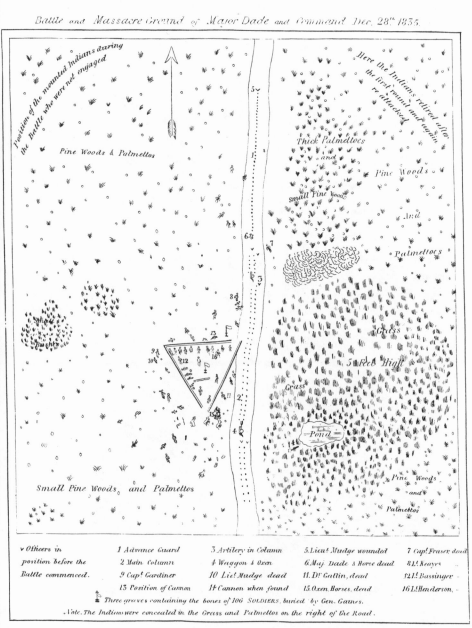

Battle and Massacre Ground of Major Dade and Command Dec. 28th 1835.

Position of the mounted Indians during the Battle who were not engaged

Pine Woods & Palmettos

Here the Indians retired after the first round and again re attacked

Thick Palmettoes and small Pine Woods

Pine Woods

And

Palmettoes

Bushes

Grass 5 Feet High

Grass

Pond

Small Pine Woods and Palmettos

Pine Woods and Palmettos

✓ Officers in	1 Advance Guard	3 Artilery in Colamn	5. Lieut Mudge wounded	7 Capt Fraser dead
position before the	2 Main Column	4 Waggon & Oxen	6. Maj. Dade & Horse dead	8 Lt Keays
Battle commenced.	9 Capt Gardiner	10 Lieut Mudge dead	11. Dr Gatlin, dead	12 Lt Bassinger
	13 Position of Cannon	14 Cannon when found	15 Oxen Horses, dead	16 Lt Henderson.

Three graves containing the bones of 106 SOLDIERS, buried by Gen. Gaines.

Note. The Indians were concealed in the Grass and Palmettos on the right of the Road.

WOODBURNE POTTER, WAR IN FLORIDA

Potter's map, made eight weeks after the massacre.

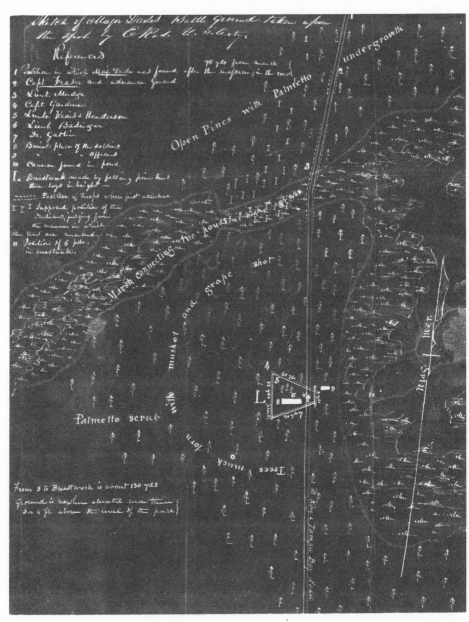

Map drawn by Lieutenant Edwin Rose, January, 1837, a year after the battle.

LECTURES.

MR. RANSOM CLARK,

The only survivor of Major Dade's

ill-fated command in Florida, proposes to deliver   lectures of the
above character at   on
at   o'clock, in the evening,   th, **1839.**

Mr. CLARK was employed to carry the U. S. Mail from Fort
Brook to Fort King ; taken prisoner by the *Seminoles*, and held in captivity *eight months* ;
escaped by killing *seven Indians* who were left to guard him ; resumed his post as mail
carrier, with a guard of 116 men, under the command of the gallant *Major Dade*, who
were *massacred* by the *Indians*, December, 28th, 1835.   During the engagement, *Mr. Clark*
was severely wounded, the marks of which he now bears upon his person, and have been
exhibited to respectable persons in this place.   He has also abundant certificates from officers of the army and others to substantiate his tale of blood and suffering.

His lectures will embrace a description of the *local scenery* of the
country which has been so long the theatre of a sanguinary contest, with the *fate* of his
comrades in that *horrid massacre*, and a sketch of the *disastrous campaigns* of 1835 and
1836,—and in connexion he will relate his own adventures,

> " Wherein he'll speak of most disastrous chances,
> Of moving accidents by flood and field,
> Of hair-breath 'scapes i' the imminent deadly breach
> Of being taken by the savage foe
> And held in slavery ; of his escape from thence,
> And with it all his travel's history."

Ladies and gentlemen are respectfully invited to attend.

Tickets, **12½** *cents, to be had at*

Poster used by Ransom Clarke to draw audiences to his lectures on the
massacre.

THE BATTLEGROUND

O N JANUARY 28, 1905, the Honorable Stephen M. Sparkman, a resident of Tampa and representative in
Congress from Florida, wrote to Brigadier General Ains-
worth, Secretary of War, asking that he send him copies of
all the files (if not too voluminous) that related to "Dade's
Massacre in Florida" seventy years before.[1] A leisurely study
of the official reports eventually produced a bill which
Representative Sparkman presented to the House on
April 19, 1911, to provide "for the marking and protection
of the battlefield known as 'Dade's Massacre,' in Sumter
County, Florida, and for the erection of a monument
thereon."[2] The bill failed to pass as did a subsequent bill
presented by Representative Sparkman four years later.

At that time the project was assumed by Senator Duncan
U. Fletcher of Florida who continued gathering documents
concerning Dade and his command. In 1921 he received
additional material and a note of encouragement from the
Superintendent of West Point, General Douglas MacArthur.
"The incident of the massacre . . . has been one of the
Army's campfire stories for a generation," MacArthur
wrote.[3]

While the papers shuffled in Washington a Dade Memo-

1. Records of the Office of the Adjutant General, Document File No. 970418,
N.A.R.S.
2. *Ibid.* The battlefield is located in township 21S, range 22E, section 20.
3. *Ibid.*

rial Association had been formed in Bushnell, Florida (a small town two miles from the battlefield). In 1921, spurred by the efforts of historical-minded Floridians, the state legislature appropriated funds for the purchase of eighty acres of land that included the site of the battle for preservation as a historic memorial. Finally the sad and silent field of battle was rescued from both obscurity and exploitation.[4]

Through the succeeding years Dade Battlefield Memorial Park has been carefully developed. The natural beauty of the area has been maintained, watched over now by giant oaks which were slender young trees when Francis Dade was buried at their feet. A replica of the log barricade has been constructed and though somewhat smaller than the original, it gives the feeling of hasty and inadequate defense within which fifty brave men fought to their last charge of powder. An interpretive museum stands just west of the last redoubt, presenting a fascinating display of the type of weapons employed in the battle, a few items belonging to William Basinger, portraits of Osceola and other Indians, and many related letters, papers, and relics of the battle. Within the acreage maintained now by the Florida Board of Parks and Historic Memorials but set apart from the battle area are picnic facilities and recreation areas. But in spite of occasional crowds and the paved roads, tennis courts and the shouts and laughter, there is still a certain quiet solemnity about the section of the Fort King Road and the graves within the low log fort.

Through the years of negotiation concerning the establishment of the park there had always been some question as to the exact location of the final struggle and subsequent burial. The remains had been removed in July, 1842, and since then the dirt-filled graves had been untouched. With the purchase by the state of the entire area of the battle, questions arose as to whether the depression near the pond had really held the bodies of Dade and his command. These questions persisted until March, 1964, when permission was

4. *Ibid.*

granted by the Park Board for members of the Florida Historical Society to excavate the assumed site of the grave.[5]

The task was begun on March 6. Screening boxes were set up and each shovelful of dirt was carefully examined through two days of digging. By evening of the second day two complete graves had been uncovered, their outlines clearly apparent in profile against the natural and untouched earth beside them. Proof of the location was abundant. Within the two graves were found a total of 315 military buttons of the type used by the army during the 1830's, the artillery A still legible. In addition, 25 lead balls were found on the floor of the graves, their only possible route here being the bodies of the men in whom they had lodged during the battle one hundred and twenty-eight years before.

Before beginning the dig, it had been assumed that the men had been buried in their uniforms as McCall and other writers had stated that most of the clothing was still on the bodies. The remains had rested here for some six years, the exhumation taking place when nothing would have been left of the bodies except bone. When these were taken up, the remaining scraps of their uniforms, with buttons attached, and the lead balls that had been in the bodies would have been left lying loose here and there in the tumbled earth. At the time of burial, the bodies had been placed on the *bottom* of the graves; therefore, the buttons and lead balls should be on the bottom also. And so they were.

All items found in the two graves were turned over to the park authorities and sent by them to the Gainesville office of the Board of Parks to be cleaned and mounted. Today they form part of the display in the park museum.

This author was privileged to take part in the excavation —the final step on the long trail of Francis Dade and his doomed command. To stand in the damp and crumbling

5. Correspondence between Mr. Bill Miller, Director, Florida Board of Parks and Historic Memorials, and William Goza, President of Florida Historical Society during February and March, 1964.

grave, surrounded by the almost tangible presence of the brave men whose dust lay in my hand, to see at my feet the buttons that rested over their pounding hearts in that last, desperate hour was a thrilling and emotional moment. If those who have read their story can share a measure of the author's satisfaction, the search has been well repaid.

THE MEN OF
DADE'S COMMAND

SOLDIER	BIRTHPLACE	AGE (AT BATTLE)	OCCUPATION
FOURTH INFANTRY REGIMENT			
Bvt. Maj. Dade, Francis Langhorne	King George County, Va.	43	pro. soldier
Detached from Company B:			
Sgt. Thomas, Peter	Philadelphia, Pa.	34	pro. soldier
Pvt. Barnes, John	Caren, Ireland	31	laborer
Pvt. Campbell, Daniel	Inverness, Scotland	35	tailor
Pvt. Cates, Enoch	Orange, N.C.	29	laborer
Pvt. Cunningham, Martin	Philadelphia, Pa.	33	clerk
Pvt. Donovan, Cornelius	Cork, Ireland	22	laborer
Pvt. Doughty, John	Dutchess, N.Y.	32	printer
Pvt. Downs, William	Baltimore, Md.	22	laborer
Pvt. Hall, Samuel	Belfast, Ireland	25	laborer
Pvt. Jones, Willie	Wake, N.C.	34	laborer
Pvt. Markham, John	Amherst, Va.	36	carpenter
SECOND ARTILLERY REGIMENT			
Capt. Gardiner, George Washington	Washington, D.C.	(?) 42	pro. soldier
1st. Lt. Basinger, William Elon	Savannah, Ga.	29	pro. soldier
Bvt. 2nd Lt. Henderson, Richard	Jackson, Tenn.	19	pro. soldier
Detached from Company B:			
Pvt. Boston, Edward	Lanarkshire, Scotland	31	clerk
Pvt. Clarke, Ransom	Livingston, N.Y.	23	drummer
Pvt. De Courcy, Edwin	Maidstone, England	27	laborer
Pvt. Kenny, Michael	Armagh, Ireland	23	blacksmith
Pvt. Laughlin, Anthony	Sligo, Ireland	27	laborer
Pvt. McCartney, John	Longford, Ireland	22	laborer
Pvt. McDonald, James	Clare, Ireland	24	laborer
Pvt. McWiggin, John	Monaghan, Ireland	21	laborer
Pvt. Peery, Hugh	Down, Ireland	28	laborer
Pvt. Roney, Patrick	Sligo, Ireland	38	laborer
Pvt. Thomas, John	Dorchester, Mass.	34	wheelwright

177

MASSACRE!

Detached from Company H:

Pvt. Bowen, Richard R.	New York, N.Y.	30	clerk
Pvt. Brondon, Henry	Hoffendorff, Prussia	39	laborer
Pvt. Craig, John	Antrim, Ireland	30	farmer
Pvt. Kerins, John	Migow, Ireland	30	hatter
Pvt. McMee, Hugh	Tyrone, Ireland	25	laborer
Pvt. Patton, John A.	Alexandria, Va.	35	barber
Pvt. Phillips, Reuben	Philadelphia, Pa.	25	laborer
Pvt. Stafford, John	Leicestershire, England	22	laborer
Pvt. Taylor, Hiram	York, Pa.	23	laborer
Pvt. Thornton, Thomas	Kingston, Canada	22	spinner
Pvt. Wright, William	Boston, Mass.	25	farmer

Company C:

1st. Sgt. Hood, John	Edinburgh, Scotland	29	plasterer
Sgt. Cooper, Philip	Coburg, Germany	42	pro. soldier
Sgt. Lovis, John	Burlington, N.J.	40	laborer
Sgt. Savin, Thomas	Antrim, Ireland	29	laborer
Cpl. Clark, Nicholas	Laurens, N.Y.	25	farmer
Cpl. Dunlap, James	Cumberland, Me.	26	clerk
Cpl. Ryan, Michael	Ireland	23	laborer
Pvt. Barton, Rufus	Ulster, N.Y.	31	laborer
Pvt. Black, William	Baltimore, Md.	32	blacksmith
Pvt. Bourke, Richard	Rathkeale, Ireland	27	musician
Pvt. Boven, Owen	Westmeath, Ireland	25	laborer
Pvt. Carney, William	Londonderry, Ireland	30	clerk
Pvt. Davis, Thomas	Philadelphia, Pa.	24	blacksmith
Pvt. Gillet, Alpheas	Troy, N.Y.	19	laborer
Pvt. Grant, Isaac C.	Smithville, N.Y.	22	laborer
Pvt. Green, Robert	Baltimore, Md.	32	musician
Pvt. Haltor, John	Lancaster, Pa.	31	laborer
Pvt. Heck, Charles T.	Lancaster, Pa.	34	clerk
Pvt. Hill, Cornelius	Antrim, Ireland	26	laborer
Pvt. Holmes, William	Longford, Ireland	25	clerk
Pvt. Howard, George	Trenton, N.J.	24	farmer
Pvt. Hurley, John	Limerick, Ireland	27	laborer
Pvt. Jewell, Aaron	Windham, Vt.	24	farmer
Pvt. Knarr, Thomas	Lehigh, Pa.	24	laborer
Pvt. Mulvahal, Robert	Limerick, Ireland	27	laborer
Pvt. Neeley, William	Derry, Ireland	22	laborer
Pvt. Rafferty, Patrick	Caimford, Ireland	25	laborer
Pvt. Riley, John	Mayo, Ireland	23	laborer
Pvt. Robertson, William	Aberdeen, Scotland	31	pntr./glazier
Pvt. Schneider, Casper	Hesse, Germany	34	papermaker
Pvt. Taylor, Isaac	Anne Arundel Co., Md.	36	tailor
Pvt. Taylor, William	Mote (?) Vt.	22	laborer
Pvt. Wilson, Joseph	Sackett's Harbor, N.Y.	36	musician
Pvt. Worcester, Orville	Windsor, Vt.	35	laborer

THIRD ARTILLERY REGIMENT

Capt. Fraser, Upton S.	New York, N.Y.	(?) 41	pro. soldier
2nd. Lt. Mudge, Robert Rich	Lynn, Mass.	26	pro. soldier
Bvt. 2nd Lt. Keais, John Low	Washington, N.C.	24	pro. soldier

Company B:

Sgt. Chapman, Benjamin	Smithfield, R.I.	36	pro. soldier
Sgt. Farley, Austin W. C.	Giles, Va.	32	farmer
Sgt. Vailing, John	Germany	38	pro. soldier
Cpl. Jones, Alexander	Salem, N.J.	32	waterman
Cpl. Wells, Philander	Utica, N.Y.	26	pro. soldier
Cpl. Young, George G.	Foster, R.I.	36	farmer
Pvt. Bertram, George	Edinburgh, Scotland	24	printer
Pvt. Camasky, Patrick	Ireland	26	laborer
Pvt. Carpenter, Ben C.	Lantentown, N.Y.	36	pro. soldier
Pvt. Dodge, Samuel E.	New York, N.Y.	24	lampmaker
Pvt. Flanagan, William	Mayo, Ireland	26	printer
Pvt. Folk, John C.	Altona, Germany	23	sailor
Pvt. Hall, Jordan	Long Island, N.Y.	32	boatman
Pvt. Herlyhigh, George	Cranston, R.I.	30	laborer
Pvt. Kinkerly, Samuel	Franklin, Pa.	25	weaver
Pvt. Kneeland, Jacob	Baltimore, Md.	31	hatter
Pvt. Lemon, Samuel	Lancaster, Pa.	32	tanner
Pvt. Minton, William	Mindham, N.J.	35	shoemaker
Pvt. Mulcahy, John	Waterford, Ireland	30	laborer
Pvt. Munroe, Donald	Albany, N.Y.	31	farmer
Pvt. Randell, William D.	Pompey, N.Y.	28	farmer
Pvt. Schafer, John	Germany	26	laborer
Pvt. Senram, Henry	Hanover, Germany	27	weaver
Pvt. Sprague, Joseph	Washington, Vt.	32	farmer
Pvt. Tuck, Washington	Farmingham, Me.	27	laborer
Pvt. Vreeland, Richard	Bergen, N.J.	24	shoemaker
Pvt. Wagner, Henry	Berks, Pa.	25	carpenter
Pvt. Wechsung, Daniel	Berka, Germany	23	baker
Pvt. Welsh, Sylvester	Cumberland, Pa.	37	pro. soldier
Pvt. Williams, John	Wexford, Ireland	23	laborer
Pvt. Wright, Samuel S.	Belfast, Ireland	29	hairdresser
Pvt. Yorke, George	Farnham, England	30	teacher
Ass't Surg. Gatlin, John Slade	Kinston, N.C. (?)	29	physician
Guide Pacheco, Louis	New Switzerland, Fla.	35	slave

Three unknown soldiers

This list was compiled by the author from the "Registers of Enlistments in the United States Army, 1798-1914."

In summation (and explanation) this indicates a total of seven officers plus Dr. Gatlin made up the group in the command. Non-commissioned officers and enlisted men seem to total one hundred and two in addition to Pacheco. The preceding list however names only ninety-nine, the remaining three being unknown. These three men are assumed here to have joined the command the first night, bringing the three additional horses with the cannon. Belton states ". . . I . . . ordered the purchase of three horses and harness and it joined the column at nine that night." The purpose of the horses was of course the rescue of the cannon and it seems likely that more than one man would have been required to handle the delivery of horses, especially since the animals had to be harnessed to the cannon (in the dark) and driven on to the major. No mention is made in any account so far found of this unknown soldier, or soldiers, returning to the fort. That this man, or men, remained with the command strikes the author as the most likely explanation of subsequent statements by Belton (March 25, 1836) and Captain E. A. Hitchcock (February 22, 1836) that the remains of *ninety-eight* noncoms and enlisted men were placed in the graves. Considering that the command (excluding officers and Pacheco) numbered ninety-nine when they left Fort Brooke, and that Thomas, Clarke, Sprague, and De Courcy escaped death on the field of battle, then three more bodies were interred than can be accounted for on the roster of the original command. Whoever brought the cannon could logically account for the three additional dead. Why they were never mentioned (assuming this hypothesis to be correct) remains a mystery.

BIBLIOGRAPHY

O NLY THOSE documents are listed here which have been found to contain material truly pertinent to this history, whether in fact, background, or cause. A great deal of material, unmentioned here, has been examined minutely but found to be lacking in verification. Much of the material, listed and unlisted, is in the possession of this author and readily available to any serious researcher who may apply.

NEWSPAPERS

Dade City (Fla.) *Banner*, 1923, "Pasco County Thirty Years Ago."
Austin (Texas) *Commercial Journal*, August, 1861.
The Charleston *Courier*, January 20, 1836; March 11, 1836; March 14, 1836; April 13, 1836; August (no date), 1836.
St. Augustine *Florida Herald*, August 15, 1842.
Pensacola *Gazette and West Florida Advertiser*, April 15, 1826; December 14, 1827; September 2, 1848.
St. Augustine *News*, August 20, 1842.
Newborn (N.C.) *Spectator*, February 26, 1836.
Richmond *Times Dispatch*, March 6, 1910.

MANUSCRIPT MATERIAL

MAPS
Duncan, Lieutenant James, Map of Dade battleground (1836), West Point Library.
Geological Survey: Tampa, Sulpher Springs, Thonotosassa, Antioch, Zephyrhills, Dade City, Lacoochee, St. Catherine, Wahoo, and Bushnell quadrangles; United States Department of the Interior, 1943-58.
Johnson, Lieutenant J. E., Battleground of Major Dade (1836), American State Papers, Military Affairs, Vol. VII.
Potter, Woodburne, Map of Dade battleground (1836).
Rose, Lieutenant Edwin, Sketch of Dade's Battleground (1837), National Archives, Record Group 77, L 75 flat.

181

Township Plats and Field Notes: T 29S, R 18E; T 29S, R 19E; T 28S, R 19E; T 28S, R 20E; T 28S, R 21E; T 27S, R 21E; T 26S, R 21E; T 25S, R 21E; T 24S, R 21E; T 23S, R 21E; T 22S, R 21E; T 22S, R 22E; T 21S, R 22E with accompanying field notes. Original government survey of Florida, obtained from Department of Agriculture, Tallahassee.

PUBLIC RECORDS

Census Rolls, Escambia County, Florida, 1840-1850-1860.
Dade, Amanda M., Application for pension, HR Report 667, 26 Cong., 1 sess., July 10, 1840; HR Report 532, 30 Cong. 1 sess., April 26, 1848.
File of marked graves, Livingston County prior to 1885, Genesee, New York.
Monthly Post Returns, National Archives, Army and Air Corps Branch, Microcopy 617, roll 147 (Fort Brooke).
Nourse, Dr. Benjamin F., mention in letter, HR Report 278, January 8, 1836, p. 31.
Registers of Enlistments in the United States Army, 1798-1914, National Archives, Army and Air Corps Branch, Microcopy M233, rolls 19 and 20.
Service Records of Officers and Men, National Archives, Navy and Military Service Branch.
Uniforms of the United States Army, Groups 4 and 5, H. A. Ogden, artist.
Uniform Regulations, National Archives, Adjutant General's Office, Record G. 94; Article 65 of 1825—Uniform and Dress of the Army, Paragraphs 321 and 822 through 868 inclusive; Article 52 of 1836—Uniform and Dress of the Army, Orders No. 36, Adjutant General's Office, May 23, 1829; No. 50, Adjutant General's Office, June 11, 1832; No. 89, Adjutant General's Office, October 13, 1832; No. 10, Adjutant General's Office, February 8, 1833; No. 38, Adjutant General's Office, May 2, 1833; No. 36, Adjutant General's Office, 1839.
Weather Diary, Fort Brooke, Florida; Asheville, North Carolina, Environmental Science Services Administration.

PERSONAL RECORDS

Basinger, William Starr, "Personal Reminiscences of William Starr Basinger, 1827-1910" and Appendices I through VI. University of Georgia Library.
Duncan, Lieutenant James, Diary (February-March, 1836). United States Military Academy Library.

PUBLISHED MATERIAL

Alvord, Benjamin, An Address Before the Dialectic Society of the Corps of Cadets of West Point, New York, 1839.
American State Papers, Vol. VI, Washington, 1861.
Army and Navy Chronicle, Vols. II, III, and V, Washington, 1835-1842.
Barr, Captain James, A Correct and Authentic Narrative of the Indian War in Florida, New York, 1836.
Bemrose, John, Reminiscences of the Second Seminole War, ed. John K. Mahon, Gainesville, 1966.
Blanchard, D. F., An Authentic Narrative of the Seminole War, Providence, 1836.
Boyd, Mark F., Florida Aflame, Tallahassee, 1951.
Boynton, Edward C., History of West Point, New York, 1863.
Browne, Jefferson B., Key West: The Old and the New, St. Augustine, 1912.
Campbell, J. Duncan, and Howell, Edgar M., American Military Insignia, Washington, 1963.
Carter, Clarence E. (ed.), Territorial Papers of the United States, Vols. XXII-XXVI (Florida Territory), Washington, 1956-62.

Centennial of the United States Military Academy at West Point, New York, The, Vol. I, HR Report 789, 58 Cong., 2 sess., Washington, 1902.

Clarke, Ransom, *The Surprising Adventures of Ransom Clarke Among the Indians in Florida,* Binghamton, N.Y., 1839.

Coe, Charles H., *Red Patriots,* Cincinnati, 1898.

Cohen, Myer M., *Notices of Florida and the Campaigns,* Gainesville, 1964 (Reprint).

Columbian Atlas of the World We Live In, The, New York, 1893.

Covington, Dr. James W., "Life at Fort Brooke, 1824-1836," *FHQ,* XXXVI (April, 1958), 319-30.

Cullum, George Washington, *Biographical Register of Graduates and Former Cadets of the United States Military Academy,* West Point, N.Y., 1960.

Doherty, Herbert J., *Richard Keith Call: Southern Unionist,* Gainesville, 1961.

Dovell, Junius E., *Florida: Historic, Dramatic, Contemporary,* New York, 1952.

Farr, Cynthia K., *Tampa's Earliest Living Pioneer: A Sketch From the Life of Mrs. Nancy Jackson,* Tallahassee, Florida, 1900.

Frederick, Davis T., "Early Orange Culture in Florida and the Epochal Cold of 1835," *FHQ,* XV (April, 1937), 232-39.

Giddings, Joshua R., *The Exiles of Florida,* Gainesville, 1964 (Reprint).

Grismer, Karl H., *Tampa: A History of the City of Tampa and the Tampa Bay Region of Florida,* St. Petersburg, 1950.

Heitman, Francis B., *Historical Register and Dictionary of the United States Army . . . to March 2, 1903,* 2 Vols., Urbana, Illinois, 1965 (Reprint).

Hitchcock, Ethan Allen, *Fifty Years in Camp and Field,* New York, 1909.

James, Marquis, *The Life Of Andrew Jackson,* New York, 1938.

Laumer, Frank, "This Was Fort Dade," *FHQ,* XLV (July, 1966), 1-11.

Lawton, Edward P., *A Saga of the South,* Ft. Myers Beach, 1965.

Long, Ellen Call, *Florida Breezes,* Gainesville, 1962 (Reprint).

McCall, George A., *Letters From the Frontiers,* Philadelphia, 1868.

McKay, D. B., *Pioneer Florida,* Vols. I and II, Tampa, 1959.

McReynolds, Edwin C., *The Seminoles,* Norman, Oklahoma, 1957.

Mahon, John K., *History of the Second Seminole War,* Gainesville, Florida, 1967.

Manucy, Albert, *Artillery Through the Ages,* Washington, 1949.

Motte, Jacob Rhett, *Journey Into Wilderness,* Gainesville, 1953.

Niles' Weekly Register, Baltimore, 1811-49.

"Osceola Issue," *FHQ,* XXXIII (January, April, 1955). The entire issue (both numbers), by various writers, is devoted to Osceola.

Ott, Eloise Robinson, and Chazel, Louis Hickman, *Ocali Country,* Ocala, Florida, 1966.

Patrick, Rembert W., *Aristocrat in Uniform: General Duncan L. Clinch,* Gainesville, 1963.

Peithmann, Irvin M., *The Unconquered Seminole Indians,* St. Petersburg, 1957.

Porter, Kenneth W., "Three Fighters for Freedom," *The Journal of Negro History,* XXVIII (January, 1943), 65-72.

Potter, Woodburne, *The War in Florida,* Baltimore, 1836.

Record of Officers and Soldiers Killed in Battle and Died in Service During the Florida War, Washington, D.C., 1882.

Register of Graduates and Former Cadets United States Military Academy, Branham, Charles N. (ed.), West Point, 1960.

Richard, Dr. James (ed.), *A Compilation of the Messages and Papers of the Presidents,* Vol. III, Washington, 1904.

Roberts, Albert H., "The Dade Massacre," *FHQ,* V (January, 1927), 123-38.

Rodenbough, Theophilus F., *From Everglade to Cañon with the Second Dragoons,* New York, 1875.

Silver, James W., *Edmund Pendleton Gaines: Frontier General*, Baton Rouge, 1949.

Smith, W. W., *Sketch of the Seminole War*, Charleston, 1836.

Sprague, John T., *The Origin, Progress, and Conclusion of the Florida War*, Gainesville, 1964 (Reprint).

United States Military Reservations, National Cemeteries, and Military Parks, Washington, 1916.

Van Every, Dale, *Disinherited: The Lost Birthright of the American Indian*, New York, 1966.

White, Frank F., Jr. (ed.), "Macomb's Mission to the Seminoles," *FHQ*, XXXV (October, 1956), 130-93.

Williams, John L., *The Territory of Florida*, Gainesville, 1962 (Reprint).

INDEX

ABRAHAM (interpreter), 19, 21, 75, 159
Alachua: Road, 48; settlers, 65
Albany, N.Y., 167
Alligator, 15, 17, 58, 60, 63, 125, 139, 148
Alvord, Lt. Benjamin: described, 9; returns to Ft. Brooke, 40; discussion of, 14; mentioned, 42, 43, 163
Arbuckle, Brig. Gen. Matthew, 18, 19
Arkansas, 15, 17, 18
Arkansas River, 18, 62
Austin, Texas, 170

BASINGER, FRANCIS K., 5, 73
Basinger, Lt. William E.: described, 3, 4; mentioned, 2, 101, 131, 138, 139, 140, 141, 146, 147, 148, 150, 154, 160, 161, 163
Baton Rouge, La., 104
Beaufort, N.C., 85
Belton, Capt. Francis S.: message to, 40; sends cannon, 43; mentioned, 1, 5, 8, 10, 11, 34, 36, 38, 42, 46, 68, 69, 70, 72, 73, 74, 75, 77, 95, 96, 127, 132, 133, 158, 159, 160, 161, 163, 164
Belton, Mrs., 47
Boston, Mass., 168
Bridges: discussion of, 38
Brooke, Col. George M., 32, 104, 105, 106, 107
"Bruce's Address," 164

CALLAVA, DON JOSE, 103, 104
Canadian River, 18
Cannon: time of arrival in camp, 43, 43n; thrown in pond, 148-49
Casey, Capt. John C.: hires Pacheco, 38; mentioned, 1, 169
Cedar Key, Fla., 165

Chandler, Lt., 52
Charley Emathla: subchief, 26; executed, 71; mentioned, 19, 23, 24, 64, 67
Cherokees, 18
Chickasaws, 18
Chocachatti, 108
Choctaws, 18
Clarke, Pvt. Ransom: described, 3; crossing of Big Withlacoochee, 111; narrative of, 167; mentioned, 2, 32, 51, 54, 55, 115, 119, 129, 136, 140, 141, 142 144, 145, 147, 148, 150, 152, 153, 155, 156, 157, 158, 160, 162, 163, 166
Clinch, Gen. Duncan L.: commanding U.S. forces, 21; orders forts reoccupied, 29; calls assembly of chiefs, 57; meeting with chiefs, 58; mentioned, 6, 46, 47, 60, 67, 76, 97, 99, 133, 159, 161, 162
Coa Hadjo, 19
Collar, Levi, 12
Collar, Nancy, 10, 12
Comanches, 18
Cooper, Sgt. Philip, 2, 8, 44
Creeks, 18, 19
Crueger, Capt., 69

DADE AMANDA M., 1, 129, 170
Dade, Fannie L., 108, 129, 170, 171
Dade, Brevet Maj. Francis L.: ancestry, sources on, 9; appearance, 10; experience, 30; abandons cannon, 34; sends Pacheco ahead, 37; sends Jewell to Ft. Brooke, 69; marriage, 108; mentioned, vii, viii, xx, 11, 13, 14,

185